JACK DANIEL'S

The Spirit of Tennessee

COOKBOOK

JACK DANIEL'S

The Spirit of Tennessee

COOKBOOK

Lynne Tolley

Pat Mitchamore

RUTLEDGE HILL PRESS®

Nashville, Tennessee

A Thomas Nelson Company

Published by Rutledge Hill Press, a Thomas Nelson Company, P. O. Box 141000, Nashville, Tennessee 37214.

Photograph on pages 46-47 (bottom right) by Jim Braddy.

Photographs on pages 17, 22 (bottom left), 23 (top right), 31 (bottom right), 44 (left and top right), 53, 64, 92-3 (top right, bottom left), 102-103 (top left), 104, 146, 149, 151, and 152-153 (top left, top right, bottom left) copyright by Joe Clark, HBSS, and reprinted by permission.

Photographs on pages 13, 14 (bottom left), 20, 25, 29 (left), 42 (left and right), 44 (bottom right), 46 (top right, bottom left), 47 (top left), 49, 60, 69 (top right), 86, 100, 108, 112, 117, 127 (bottom right), 128, 139, 142, 153 (bottom right), 163, 167, 170, and 171 copyright by Junebug Clark and reprinted by permission.

Photographs on pages 39, 40, 81, and 180 by Bob Freson.

Photograph on page 48 by Joel Harris.

Photographs on pages 14-15 (top left, top right, bottom right), 22-23 (top middle, bottom right), 35, 43, 46 (top left), 50, 54, 58, 62-63 (top left, bottom left, bottom middle, bottom right), 65, 68-69 (top left, bottom right), 72, 84 (top left, top middle), 89, 92-93 (top left, bottom right), 96, 102-103 (top right, bottom left, bottom right), 106 (left, right), 111, 114-115 (top left, top right, bottom left, bottom right), 122, 127 (top right), 129, 133, 136-137 (top left, top right, bottom left, bottom middle, bottom right), 141, 144 (left, right), 148, 156, 157, 161, 165, 168-169 (bottom right), 172, 173, and 176 copyright by Robin Hood and reprinted by permission.

Photographs on pages 125 and 140 by Slick Lawson.

Photographs on pages 29 (right), 82 and 134 by Archie Lieberman.

Photograph on pages 114-115 (top middle) by Pat Mitchamore.

Photographs on pages 85 (bottom) and 103 (bottom left) by Norm Parker.

Photographs on pages 30-31 (bottom left, top right) by Hope Powell.

Photographs on pages 76 (top) and 77 (top) by Mike Rutherford.

Photographs on pages 126-127 (top left, bottom left), 168-169 (top left, top right, bottom left), and 177 (left, top right, top left) courtesy of State of Tennessee Photographic Services.

Food styling for jacket photograph by Mary Ann Fowlkes.

Jacket and text design by Harriette Bateman.

Typography by Bailey Typography, Nashville, Tennessee

Library of Congress Cataloging-in-Publication Data

Tolley, Lynne, 1950-
  Jack Daniel's the Spirit of Tennessee cookbook / Lynne Tolley, Pat Mitchamore.
     p.   cm.
  Includes index.
  ISBN 1-558-53001-0
  1. Cookery (Whiskey)   I. Mitchamore, Pat, 1934- II. Title.
TX726.T65   1988   88-22746
641.6′25—dc19   CIP

Printed in the United States of America
9 10 11 — 05 04 03 02 01 00

CONTENTS

FOREWORD

Since that day in 1904 when Mr. Jack Daniel won a gold medal at the St. Louis World's Fair for his Tennessee Sour Mash Sippin' Whiskey, his Old No. 7 has been *the* spirit of Tennessee. The state of Tennessee, with the rugged Great Smoky Mountains on the east, the wide and mighty Mississippi on the west and the gently rolling hills in the middle, emanates a spirit as rich in heritage and tradition as in variety and flavor. It is these combined ingredients that we have sought to portray in this book.

Tennessee's spirit has come mostly from the people, those who struggled against the high mountain range to settle here. It took determination and strong bodies to cross the majestic mountains in the east. They had pulled up roots from their homelands, and particles of those places and their past clung to them as they made their home in a new land.

Tennessee has three distinctly different regions. The lay of the land in many ways depicts the spirit of the people who settled each region. Those who stayed in the mountains were rugged, tenacious, private and proud of their highland heritage. Those settling in the flat and open Mississippi Delta land were as diverse as the ports and ships that traversed the great river. They were gregarious, open-minded and openly faced the frontier beyond. Those who settled in the middle were a composite of the other two. They bridged the gap, tying east and west together. They came seeking new challenges and new frontiers, but brought the joys of their past into a present which promised a wider and broader horizon.

The foods that evolved from the diverse peoples, the available produce and the new products brought from homelands to a new country are interesting, nurturing and delicious. Today they are a blending of the best of the past with the present, lovingly passed down to our generation. This is not new cuisine, rather it is a collection of favorites that have evolved and expanded from those of past generations. Here is southern food at its regional best.

Whiskey has traditionally been served as a celebration drink for special occasions and social gatherings. Most homes also kept a bottle for use as medicine or tonic. People are now more imaginative. Today inventive cooks and chefs use Jack Daniel's as a flavorful ingredient in the preparation of favorite dishes. They have created rich and delicious new sauces, side dishes, entrées and desserts. We have included some of these to round out our collection of cherished favorites.

Tennessee is renowned for many things, most notably its music, scenic beauty, walking horses and Jack Daniel's Whiskey. Our guests represent the cultures and traditions of almost every country in the world. Many of the international visitors have become familiar with Tennessee because of Jack Daniel's Whiskey. The millions of visitors annually leave extolling Tennesseans for their food and hospitality.

This book is our portrait of the state, the people and their industry. We have tried to depict the prevailing rich spirit that emanates from music, traditions, way of life, manner of hospitality, and, most certainly, in the food that they prepare and enjoy. That is the spirit of this book!

JACK DANIEL'S

The Spirit of Tennessee

COOKBOOK

DRINKS

AIRPORT

   1 jigger Jack Daniel's Whiskey
    Juice of ½ orange
   1 dash lemon juice
    Asti Spumante wine
    Orange slice

Combine Jack Daniel's Whiskey and juices in glass. Top with Asti Spumante; garnish with a slice of orange. Makes 1 serving.

AMBER JACK

   1 part Jack Daniel's Whiskey
  ½ part Amaretto liqueur
   2 parts bottled sweet and sour mix
    Maraschino cherries

Combine first 3 ingredients; serve over cracked ice. Garnish with a cherry. Makes 1 serving.

AUTHENTIC JACK DANIEL'S MOORE COUNTY MIST

    Lemon twist
  2½ ounces Jack Daniel's Whiskey

Pack your favorite 6-ounce tumbler with finely crushed ice; rub the rim with a lemon twist and place twist on top of ice. Pour 2½ ounces of Jack Daniel's Whiskey over the ice. Sip slowly as your glass frosts and enjoy the whiskey from the hills of Tennessee that's charcoal mellowed drop-by-drop for smoothness. Makes 1 serving.

11

*

On a trip to Europe, Mark Twain assured the customs inspector that his bag contained nothing but clothing. As if failing to hear, the customs inspector searched his bags and found a bottle of bourbon.

Facing him the customs man said, "I thought that you said there was only clothing in here."

"I did," replied Twain. "You're looking at my night cap!"

*

Black Raider

2 ounces Jack Daniel's Whiskey
½ ounce Triple Sec
1 ounce lemon juice
1 dash Grenadine
Orange slices

Combine first 4 ingredients; serve over cracked ice. Garnish with an orange slice. Makes 1 serving.

Bowl Game Punch

2 cups boiling water
1 tablespoon maple syrup
¼ teaspoon cinnamon
¼ teaspoon nutmeg
1 tablespoon bitters
1 (750 ml) bottle dry red wine
1 orange, studded with cloves
2 cups Jack Daniel's Whiskey

Combine first 6 ingredients and heat just to boiling, but do not boil. Keep warm, without boiling. Float orange over top of spiced wine mixture. Just before serving add Jack Daniel's Whiskey. Makes approximately 2 quarts.

Bride's Party Punch

Juice of 6 lemons
2 tablespoons sugar
¼ cup Curacao liqueur
1 (750 ml) bottle Jack Daniel's Whiskey
1 quart soda or iced tea
Fresh fruit, sliced

Combine all ingredients except fruit. Pour over ice-filled punch bowl. Stir and garnish with fruit. Makes approximately 2 quarts.

Broken Leg
(Cold weather drink)

5 ounces hot apple juice
1 ounce Jack Daniel's Whiskey
Cinnamon stick
Lemon slice

Combine liquid ingredients in a mug and stir. Garnish with cinnamon stick and slice of lemon. This may also be served cold over ice in the summertime and called a "Sunburn Tonic." Makes 1 serving.

*

A Fisherman's Toast

Here's to the fish that I may catch
So large that even I,
When talking of it afterwards,
Will never need to lie.

*

CAFE DANIEL

¼ *cup Jack Daniel's Whiskey*
2 *teaspoons brown sugar*
2 *cups espresso coffee (demitasse cup)*
  Whipped cream
  Cinnamon

Heat Jack Daniel's Whiskey with brown sugar, stirring until sugar dissolves. Add 2 cups espresso coffee; top with whipped cream and sprinkle with cinnamon. Makes 2 servings.

CELEBRATION FIZZ

1½ *ounces Jack Daniel's Whiskey*
5 *dashes lemon juice*
3 *dashes Curacao liqueur*
1 *teaspoon sugar*
1 *egg*
  Ice
  Soda water

Shake all ingredients except soda water in cocktail shaker. Strain into short glass. Fill with soda water. Makes 1 serving.

The Tennessee Hills

I n Middle Tennessee, mists rise early from the little hollows, gaps and passes in the rolling hills. The look and feel is that of a soft focus, a sensual and appealing landscape. It is undeniably Tennessee. The spring is resplendent with color—pink, rose, lilac, pristine white, and yellow. The summer is lush green, and fall is flamboyant with hues of red and gold. Winter is winter. However, in all the seasons it is the lay of the land and the mists of the morning that identify Tennessee.

Old timers talk about changes since they were kids. Outhouses have been replaced by indoor plumbing, electricity brings New York and the world into every farmhouse living room, and you see fewer "See Rock City" birdhouses along the road. The tobacco barns, which still dot the landscape, are aged and empty and falling ramshackle into the past. Once every farmer raised tobacco because it was a good money-crop, clothing the family, educating the kids and paying for maintenance of farm and machinery.

The disappearance of tobacco crops is a reminder of back when all the falderal began about prohibition. At that time making whiskey was a way of life in the South. As sure as the womenfolk canned corn, the men distilled it. Almost everybody made a little whiskey for family celebrations, enjoyment and medicinal purposes. Grain was plentiful and the iron-free spring limestone water made good whiskey.

When prohibition came people continued to make their own whiskey right beside the road, and no one seemed to take a mind. Since legal and registered distilleries had closed down, the farmers found available outlets for their homemade products. Money made during that time bought many a farm.

If you have never visited this part of the world, it bears repeating what has been said a thousand times: "Y'all come." Farmers will wave to you just as though they knew you. Food and hospitality abound. The mists will still rise in the morning in a beauty rare except in these rolling hills, and deep within you'll feel at peace with God, nature and your fellow man. This is Tennessee.

*

FOUR AND TWENTY BRITISH
FEELING VERY DRY,
SAILED ACROSS THE OCEAN
OUR WHISKEY WANT TO TRY.
WHEN OPENED THEY THE BOTTLE,
THE RED COATS THEY DID SING,
GOD BLESS AMERICA,
AND GOD SAVE THE KING.

*

CHAMPAGNE PUNCH

2 bottles champagne
1 bottle sauterne
3 cups sugar
2 cups lemon juice
4 cups canned cubed pineapple
1½ quarts ice water
1 quart strawberries
1 pint cognac

Chill champagne and sauterne thoroughly. Dissolve sugar in lemon juice, combine in punch bowl with pineapple; add a square block of ice, sauterne and ice water. Just before serving, add strawberries, chilled champagne and cognac. Makes 25 servings.

CHOCOLATE JACK

3 1-ounce squares semi-sweet chocolate
¼ cup whipping cream
3 cups hot brewed coffee
1 heaping tablespoon brown sugar
½ cup Jack Daniel's Whiskey
¼ cup crème de cacao liqueur
Whipped cream
Grated chocolate

Combine chocolate squares and ¼ cup whipping cream in top of a double boiler over boiling water. Stir until chocolate melts. Gradually add coffee and brown sugar; stir until frothy. Combine whiskey and crème de cacao; pour 2 tablespoons into each of 6 mugs. Add hot coffee mixture. Garnish with whipped cream and grated chocolate. Makes 6 servings.

DANIEL'S CIDER

1½ ounces Jack Daniel's Whiskey
Sparkling cider (Martinelli or other brand)
Cinnamon stick

Pour Jack Daniel's Whiskey into glass. Fill with cider. Add cinnamon stick. Makes 1 serving.

EGGNOG

12 eggs, separated and whites whipped stiff
1 cup sugar
1 cup milk
2 cups Jack Daniel's Whiskey (what else?)
½ teaspoon salt
3 pints heavy cream, whipped
Grated fresh nutmeg to taste

Start this recipe the night before serving. Combine all ingredients, except nutmeg, and chill until serving time. Garnish with freshly grated nutmeg. Makes approximately 2½ quarts.

FREIGHT TRAIN

Jack Daniel's Whiskey
Grand Marnier

Combine Jack Daniel's Whiskey and Grand Marnier to taste, over ice. Makes 1 serving.

FRISKY WHISKEY

⅔ cup Jack Daniel's Whiskey
1 teaspoon sugar
1 teaspoon crème de menthe liqueur
 Dash Curacao liqueur
 Ice

Combine all ingredients; shake in cocktail shaker. Strain into small stemmed glasses. Makes 3 servings.

GINGER JACK

1 part Jack Daniel's Whiskey
2 parts ginger ale
 Lemon twist

Pour ingredients over ice; stir and serve. Garnish with lemon twist. Makes 1 serving.

HOT SOUTHERN COMFORT NOG

3 cups milk
1 cup light cream or half-and-half
4 eggs, lightly beaten
2 tablespoons sugar
1 cup Southern Comfort
1 cup Jack Daniel's Whiskey
 Freshly grated nutmeg

Heat milk and cream in a medium saucepan over low heat until bubbles appear around the edge. Remove from heat and set aside. Whisk together eggs and sugar in a small bowl until thick and light yellow. Stir in Southern Comfort and Jack Daniel's Whiskey. Add about 1 cup hot milk mixture to each of four 12-ounce mugs. Divide whiskey mixture between mugs; sprinkle with nutmeg. Makes 4 servings.

HOT TODDY

 Jack Daniel's Whiskey
1 tablespoon sugar
½ lemon
 Boiling water

Use a heavy glass tumbler. Fill approximately half full with Jack Daniel's Whiskey. Add sugar. Squeeze lemon and drop into glass. Stir until sugar dissolves. Fill glass with boiling water. Makes 1 serving.

HOT WEATHER DELIGHT

1 6-ounce can frozen limeade concentrate, thawed
¾ cup Jack Daniel's Whiskey
¾ cup beer

Combine all ingredients. Serve over ice in stemmed glasses. Makes 6 servings.

JACK COLLINS

    1 6-ounce can frozen lemonade concentrate
⅓ cup Jack Daniel's Whiskey
    Soda water or tonic water
    Maraschino cherries and orange wedges

Stir lemonade concentrate with Jack Daniel's Whiskey until melted and well mixed. Pour into pitcher. Add soda or tonic water to taste. Serve in tall glasses filled with ice cubes. Garnish with cherries and orange wedges. Makes 4 to 6 servings.

JACK DANIEL'S MINT JULEP

    Sugar
    Fresh mint sprigs
2 ounces Jack Daniel's Whiskey
2 tablespoons Bols apricot brandy

Make syrup by bringing to a boil 4 parts sugar and 1 part water until thickened. Crush 1 mint sprig in a 12-ounce glass. Add 1 ounce whiskey and ¾ ounce syrup. Stir. Partially fill glass with ice; stir again and finish filling glass with ice. Float 1 tablespoon of apricot brandy on top. Garnish with wet mint sprinkled with sugar. Makes 2 servings.

JACK DANIEL'S PUNCH

Sometime during the early colonization of India, the British coined the word *punch* from the Indian word *paunch,* which means five. Traditionally, punch was made of five ingredients: citrus fruit juice, liquor, sugar, spice and water. Punch is still a national favorite and each celebration has a punch as traditional as the Christmas tree, fireworks or wedding cake.

To lift the spirits of any picnic, barbecue or other summer celebration, try Jack Daniel's Punch, a classic citrus punch!

2 (750 ml) bottles Jack Daniel's Whiskey
  Juice of 6 lemons (6 ounces)
1 18-ounce can pineapple juice
  Juice of 8 oranges (24 ounces)
2 14-ounce bottles ginger ale
  Sugar
  Orange, lemon and pineapple slices

Combine first 4 ingredients over block of ice in punch bowl. Add ginger ale and sugar to taste. Garnish with orange, lemon and pineapple slices. Makes about 45 servings.

JACK FROST

2 tablespoons Jack Daniel's Whiskey
1 tablespoon Drambuie
2 tablespoons cherry juice or Grenadine
¼ cup orange juice
¼ cup bottled sweet and sour mix
  Maraschino cherries

Combine first 5 ingredients over ice in tall glass. Garnish with a cherry. Makes 1 serving.

*

MAY YOU NEVER FORGET WHAT IS WORTH REMEMBERING OR REMEMBER WHAT IS BEST FORGOTTEN.

*

JACKIRI'

1 6-ounce can frozen limeade or lemonade concentrate
1 6-ounce can water
1 tablespoon sugar
½ cup Jack Daniel's Whiskey
  Ice

Combine all ingredients; process in electric blender. Cracked ice will produce a smoother consistency. For a thicker drink, add more ice. Serve in a stemmed glass. Makes 1 serving.

JACK SOUR

1 part Jack Daniel's Whiskey
2 parts bottled sweet and sour mix
  Maraschino cherries
  Orange slices

Combine first 2 ingredients; serve over cracked ice. Garnish with a cherry and an orange slice. Makes 1 serving.

LADIES' PREFERENCE

2 parts Jack Daniel's Whiskey
1 part white crème de menthe liqueur
  Ice

Combine all ingredients; shake in cocktail shaker. Strain into stemmed glass. Makes 1 serving.

LAZY SUSAN

1½ ounces Jack Daniel's Whiskey
1 ounce grapefruit juice
¾ ounce Grenadine
    Ice

Combine all ingredients in a cocktail shaker. Shake well and strain into a cocktail glass. Makes 1 serving.

LYNCHBURG LEMONADE

1 part Jack Daniel's Whiskey
1 part Triple Sec
1 part bottled sweet and sour mix
4 parts Sprite
    Lemon slices
    Maraschino cherries

Combine first 4 ingredients. Add ice and stir. Garnish with lemon slices and cherries. Great by the pitcher or individual glass. Makes 1 serving.

LYNCHBURG SLUSH

2 cups water
⅓ cup sugar
1 6-ounce can frozen lemonade concentrate
½ cup Jack Daniel's Whiskey
1 quart ginger ale
1 lemon, thinly sliced

In blender, combine water, sugar, lemonade and Jack Daniel's Whiskey; process until the sugar is dissolved. Transfer to a covered container and freeze (mixture will remain slushy). To serve, pour frozen mixture into 2-quart pitcher and add ginger ale. Float lemon slices on top. Makes 2 quarts, or 12 servings.

MILK PUNCH
(Green Pastures)

2 ounces Jack Daniel's Whiskey
1 ounce rum
½ ounce brandy
⅔ cup vanilla ice cream
¼ cup half-and-half
    Nutmeg for garnish

Process all ingredients, except nutmeg, in a blender until thick. Sprinkle a dash of nutmeg on top before serving. Makes 1 serving.

Mint Julep
(Jack Daniel's Style)

Confectioners' sugar
2½ ounces Jack Daniel's Whiskey
Fresh mint sprigs

Dissolve 1 teaspoon confectioners' sugar with two teaspoons water in a silver mug or collins glass. Fill with finely shaved ice and 2½ ounces Jack Daniel's Whiskey. Stir until glass is heavily frosted; add more ice if necessary. (Do not hold glass with hand while stirring). Decorate with five or six sprigs of fresh mint so that the tops are about two inches above rim of mug or glass. Use short straws so that it will be necessary to bury nose in mint. The mint is intended for odor rather than taste. Makes 1 serving.

Mr. Jack's Punch

2 (750 ml) bottles Jack Daniel's Whiskey
8 ounces Amaretto liqueur
4 ounces Grenadine
1 18-ounce can pineapple juice
24 ounces orange juice
14 ounces ginger ale

Combine all ingredients; pour over ice mold made with lime slices and red cherries. Makes about 45 servings.

Mrs. Butts' Boiled Custard

This is the traditional holiday drink in the South, and it is wonderful! Mrs. Butts shared her family's recipe. All who have tasted this swear it to be pure heaven to the taste buds.

2 quarts whole milk
1½ cups sugar
6 large eggs
2 teaspoons vanilla
Whipped cream
Jack Daniel's Whiskey

Warm milk over low heat. Mix sugar and eggs together. Add one cup of warm milk to egg/sugar mixture. Add egg/sugar mixture to rest of warm milk. Heat on low until mixture coats spoon. Strain mixture into a bowl. Add 2 teaspoons of vanilla. Keep covered in refrigerator and serve cold. Serve in punch cups with a dollop of whipped cream and a lacing of Jack Daniel's. Makes ½ gallon.

Old Fashioned

Pinch of sugar dissolved in ½ teaspoon of water
2 drops bitters
1 slice orange, halved
1 maraschino cherry
Jack Daniel's Whiskey

Combine first 4 ingredients in an old-fashioned glass. Top with Jack Daniel's Whiskey to taste. Makes 1 serving.

Orange Cordial

8 oranges
2 lemons
1 (750 ml) bottle Jack Daniel's Whiskey
1¼ cups sugar
½ cup water

Peel the zest from the fruit with a swivel-bladed potato peeler, avoiding the white pith (set fruit aside for later use). Place zest in a glass container; cover with Jack Daniel's Whiskey. Seal and place in a cool, dark area to age for 5 to 6 weeks. Strain and discard zest. Boil sugar and water until sugar dissolves. Cool to room temperature. Add to the whiskey. Seal and ripen for 4 more weeks before serving. Makes 1 quart.

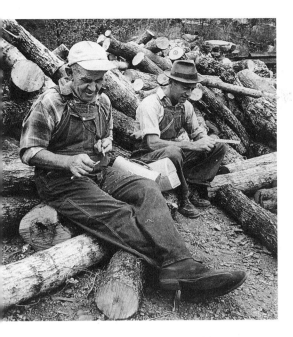

The Labor of Philosophers

N othing beats whittling for calming your nerves and inducing straight thinking. City folk might jingle their change or rattle their keys, but in Lynchburg, Tennessee, we whittle.

You don't need any fancy equipment if you have a hankering to try it. All you need is a bench somewhere in the shade (we prefer the town square), a straight-grained piece of soft wood, a sharp knife, an Arkansas oil stone to keep it sharp, and the local philosophers to join you. You know the types—those who have opinions, who have thought about things. This is Lynchburg's forum for thought and ideas. Here we contribute various bits of wisdom on such matters as world problems, how the government should be run, who's the best man to elect for road overseer and other important topics for the day. No matter how small the group, there's always a difference of opinion on most any subject. So, while your fellow philosopher expounds his ideas, you can just sit there whittling and thinking. When it comes your time, then you will have your ideas in good order.

There are two important things to remember when whittling. First, you aren't making anything but real fine curly shavings, so keep your pace slow and see how long you can make that piece of wood last. Second, keep in mind that this old world has never pleased us all and undoubtedly never will. So, do what you can to set things straight and don't get too het up . about the things you can't change.

*

MAY YOU LOOK BACK ON THE PAST
WITH AS MUCH PLEASURE
AS YOU LOOK FORWARD
TO THE FUTURE.

*

PEACH SLUSH

½ very ripe peach
1½ teaspoons sugar
Squirt of lemon juice
1½ ounces Jack Daniel's Whiskey
Crushed ice

Combine all ingredients in a blender until slushy. Serve in stemmed glass. Makes 1 serving.

PEACH SOUR

½ ripe peach, peeled
1½ ounces Jack Daniel's Whiskey
½ ounce peach liqueur
Juice of ½ lemon
1 teaspoon sugar
⅓ cup crushed ice
Peach slice

Combine first 6 ingredients in a chilled blender jar; process until almost smooth. Pour into a large chilled wine glass; garnish with a peach slice. Makes 1 serving.

SAZERAC

Pernod
1 sugar cube
3 to 4 drops bitters
Strip of lemon zest
Strip of orange zest
Crushed ice
2 ounces Jack Daniel's Whiskey

Pour enough Pernod into a low glass to coat the interior completely. Place the sugar cube in the bottom of the glass and drop the bitters onto it. Crush the sugar with the back of a spoon. Add lemon and orange zest. Fill glass two-thirds full with crushed ice. Pour Jack Daniel's Whiskey over ice and stir once. Serve. Paradise is on earth at this moment.

SNOW SHOE

2 parts Jack Daniel's Whiskey
1½ parts peppermint schnapps

Pour over crushed ice. Makes 1 serving.

SOUTHERN SLUSH

2 cups Jack Daniel's Whiskey
2½ cups tea (2½ cups water and 2 small teabags)
1 12-ounce can frozen limeade concentrate, thawed
1 6-ounce can frozen orange juice concentrate, thawed
1 cup sugar
6 cups water
Maraschino cherries

Combine all ingredients except cherries. Freeze in a non-breakable container. To serve, scoop into a glass. Garnish with stemmed cherry. Makes approximately 3 quarts.

A SUPERIOR MINT JULEP

1 teaspoon sugar
2 teaspoons water
3 sprigs fresh mint
3 ounces Jack Daniel's Whiskey

Use a chilled 10-ounce glass. Throw away the sugar, the water and the mint. Pour Jack Daniel's Whiskey over ice. Drink. Makes 1 serving.

TENNESSEE JULEP

2 teaspoons sugar
4 sprigs fresh mint
2 ounces Jack Daniel's Whiskey
  Fresh mint sprigs
  Pineapple cubes
  Maraschino cherries
  Confectioners' sugar
  Peach brandy

To a 12-ounce mint julep glass, add 2 teaspoons sugar, dash of water, and 4 sprigs of fresh mint. Bruise mint thoroughly and fill glass half full with finely cracked ice. Add Jack Daniel's Whiskey. Stir, and fill glass with ice. Garnish with sprig of mint, pineapple cube and maraschino cherry. Dust mint with confectioners' sugar; add to glass. Float 1 tablespoon of peach brandy on surface of drink. The fragrance of the peach brandy as it seeks its meeting with the prince of all whiskeys, Jack Daniel's, creates a drink known and appreciated by all old-time Southern gentlemen. Makes 1 serving.

TENNESSEE MUD

Coffee
Jack Daniel's Whiskey
Amaretto

Pour coffee into cup. Add Jack Daniel's Whiskey and Amaretto to taste. Makes 1 serving.

TENNESSEE SPIRIT PUNCH

1 12-ounce can frozen lemonade concentrate
1 6-ounce can limeade concentrate
1 6-ounce can orange juice concentrate
6 cups water
1 cup sugar
2 cups Jack Daniel's Whiskey

Combine all ingredients; place in freezer. Just before it freezes, process in a blender. Serve in stemmed glasses. Makes approximately 3 quarts.

TENNESSEE-STYLE APPLE CHERRY LIQUEUR

5 16-ounce cans tart red cherries, drained and pitted
2 fresh apples, cored, quartered and unpeeled
2 cups sugar
1½ teaspoons whole allspice
1½ teaspoons whole cloves
1 cinnamon stick
4 cups Jack Daniel's Whiskey

Combine all ingredients in a 4-quart glass jar. Stir; cover. Place in a cool, dark place for at least 8 weeks. Stir daily or several times a week. Strain before serving. Serve in liqueur glasses. Makes 1 quart of delicious liqueur.

Tennessee Tom and Jerry

12 eggs, well beaten
1 cup sifted confectioners' sugar
6 jiggers (1½ ounces each) Jack Daniel's Whiskey
6 cups boiling water
Nutmeg

Combine eggs and sugar in a blender until thick. Add a jigger of whiskey to each of 6 glasses. Pour ⅔ cup boiling water into each glass. Add several tablespoons of the sugar mixture to each. Garnish with a dash of nutmeg. Serve hot. Makes 6 servings.

Tropical Fruit Sunrise

1 6-ounce can frozen pineapple juice concentrate
1 6-ounce can frozen limeade concentrate
¾ cup soda water
¾ cup Jack Daniel's Whiskey
1 banana

Place all ingredients in a blender. Add ice to fill container; blend until slushy. Makes 6 servings.

Wyooter Hooter

The hills of Tennessee are as gentle and peaceful as any place on this earth. Walking over their ridges and down their valleys can make even a bone-tired soul feel refreshed.

But beware. Here too lurks something old and evil. Go into these hills at the wrong time, on the wrong night, and your walk may end in a headlong flight from a being that haunts these hills.

We refer—dare we breathe its name—to the Tennessee Wyooter.

Few have ever seen the Tennessee Wyooter. Of those who do, few survive. And of those who do survive, few are able to tell their awful tale; a Wyooter victim may escape with his life but lose his wits and power of speech forevermore.

Yet, there are some eyewitness accounts—fearsome accounts like this one told by Lem Hopkins.

"It was just turning midnight when we started the long walk across Peabody Ridge. It was so dark I had to hang on to Lightnin' to keep up with him. This would be a night I'd always remember.

"We moved fearfully up the mountainside. There was something over the treetops. Lightnin' bristled. There could be no mistake. It towered above us . . . eyeing us hungrily . . . it was the Tennessee Wyooter all right.

"We felt the ground tremble beneath our feet. The Tennessee Wyooter had landed directly in front of us. Its eerie form, tall as a tree, was silhouetted against the dark and threatening sky. Its giant claws were extended above its head. Its feet were planted far apart, and a poisonous mist emitted from its distended nostrils. Its wild and weird eyes glowed as if it could taste us already.

"All my life flashed before me in a single instant. I knew my time had come. But as that giant paw descended, Lightnin' made one last mighty lunge that carried us both through the great arch between the old Wyooter's legs.

"Suddenly, we were in the back of that varmint. Lightnin' had bested the Tennessee Wyooter. Since Wyooters, once they've landed, can't turn around, we knew we were safe as we struck out for home.

"Ma had a feast of corn pone, sow belly and possum gravy waiting for us. I promptly wolfed it down—as I vowed never again to go up on Peabody Ridge anywhere near Halloween . . . as long as I live. Old Lightnin', I wager, has vowed the same."

1 part Jack Daniel's Whiskey
4 parts Sprite
Dash of Grenadine

Serve over ice.

APPETIZERS

ARTICHOKE SPREAD

  1 14-ounce can artichoke hearts
  1 cup grated Parmesan cheese
  ½ cup mayonnaise
  ½ cup sour cream
    Garlic salt
    Pepper

Preheat oven to 350°. Drain artichoke hearts and chop. Add cheese, mayonnaise, sour cream and seasonings to taste. Place in shallow baking dish. Bake for 20 to 25 minutes or until lightly browned. Cool for 5 to 8 minutes before serving. Serve as spread for crackers. Makes 6 servings.

BLEU CHEESE APPETIZER SPREAD

  ½ cup butter, softened
  ½ cup bleu cheese, softened
  3 tablespoons Jack Daniel's Whiskey
  ¼ cup walnuts, finely chopped

Combine butter, cheese and Jack Daniel's Whiskey in a food processor and blend until smooth. Remove from processor; stir in walnuts. Cover and chill for several hours or overnight. Serve with crackers. Makes 1 cup.

COMPANY'S AT THE FRONT DOOR CHEESE SPREAD

1 cup shredded sharp cheddar cheese
1 cup shredded Swiss or Jarlsberg cheese
¼ cup unsalted butter, softened
2 tablespoons dry sherry
1 tablespoon caraway seed

Combine cheeses and butter in food processor until smooth. Add sherry and caraway seed until blended. Serve immediately with crackers. Keeps several weeks in refrigerator. Makes 2¼ cups.

HERBED CHEESE SPREAD

1 8-ounce package cream cheese, at room temperature
1 clove garlic, minced
1 teaspoon caraway seed
1 teaspoon dried basil
1 teaspoon dried dill weed
1 teaspoon finely chopped chives
Lemon pepper

Blend all ingredients except lemon pepper. Line a small container with plastic wrap; use spatula to press cheese mixture into container. Cover and refrigerate several hours or overnight. Unmold and cover with lemon pepper. Serve with crackers. Makes 1 cup.

MOORE COUNTY CHEESE BALL

3 8-ounce packages cream cheese, softened
2 5-ounce jars sharp cheese spread
⅛ teaspoon garlic salt

¼ teaspoon liquid hickory smoke flavoring
3 tablespoons Jack Daniel's Whiskey
Chopped pecans

Mix all ingredients, except pecans. Form into two balls; roll in chopped pecans. Chill until firm. Serve with crackers. Makes 24 servings.

SHRIMP BUTTER

½ pound shrimp, cooked, shelled and deveined
2 teaspoons lemon juice
1 teaspoon anise-flavored liqueur
½ teaspoon Dijon-style mustard
¼ teaspoon salt
Dash of red pepper sauce
4 tablespoons butter
¼ cup cream cheese, softened

Using food processor with steel blade, combine shrimp, lemon juice, liqueur, mustard, salt and pepper sauce. Process until smooth, scraping bowl once. With processor running, drop butter by the tablespoon through feed tube. Add cream cheese and process until smooth. Transfer to small bowl. Cover and refrigerate for several hours to blend flavors. Serve with crackers or toast. Makes 1 cup.

DIVINE FRUIT DIP

2 cups sour cream
⅛ to ¼ cup firmly packed light brown sugar
3 to 4 tablespoons Jack Daniel's Whiskey

Blend sour cream and brown sugar until sugar is dissolved. Stir in Jack Daniel's Whiskey. Use as a dipping sauce for fresh fruit such as strawberries, green seedless grapes, or sliced apples. This is also delicious as a sauce over fresh, cubed pineapple. Garnish with a sprinkle of brown sugar. Makes 2½ cups.

Miss Mary Bobo's Boarding House

O n July 10, 1981, Mary Bobo of Lynchburg, Tennessee, turned 100 years old. The Jack Daniel Distillery had introduced "Miss Mary" in an ad a few months earlier. It mentioned that Miss Mary was to celebrate her 100th birthday and gave her address if anyone would like to drop her a card. The response was overwhelming. She received more than 7000 cards, including one from President Carter, 36 birthday cakes and many gifts. Television and local media covered her birthday, and Miss Mary properly celebrated 100 years of living.

Prior to World War II boardinghouses were a typical American establishment. Young men who left the farm for the big city, traveling salesmen and single women of all ages found a home in a new community at boardinghouses. Boardinghouses offered a homelike atmosphere with food shared at a large table and served family style. Big breakfasts, midday dinner (not lunch) and evening supper were the three meals served. Room and three meals a day could cost up to $15.00 per week, a handsome sum but worth it for the right place. A boardinghouse offered the comforts of home, respectability, the support of others in the absence of real family, plus a cleaned room and meals.

Jack and Mary Bobo purchased their house in 1908 from the family of Dr. E. Y. Salmon, who had recently died. Dr. Salmon had built the house in 1857, one-half block off the town square. The Bobos opened a boardinghouse and called it the Bobo Hotel. Eventually, this was changed to the Bobo Boarding House.

Jack Bobo died in 1948 and Mary Bobo continued the boardinghouse until her death in 1983—she was one month shy of her 102nd birthday. Until she was 98 years old, Miss Mary lived alone, planned the meals, ordered groceries, oversaw the kitchen and other help and paid all the bills.

A few years before she died, she stopped taking roomers and started serving midday dinner only. Food was still typical boardinghouse fare: two meats, many vegetables and side dishes, homemade breads, desserts and beverage. The food was simple, abundant and delicious.

Miss Mary Bobo's Boarding House was talked about far and wide for the delicious meals of typical southern food. Fried chicken, catfish, meat loaf, pot roast, country ham were all prepared the old-fashioned way. Vegetables picked fresh from the garden in the morning were cooked for dinner. Especially good were the fried okra, fried corn, snap beans, fresh peas and stewed tomatoes. Desserts rich with cream and eggs or fresh with berries, peaches, apples or pears were served to finish every meal.

When Miss Mary died, Lynne Tolley took over the boardinghouse and continued the tradition. She runs it as a restaurant, serving midday dinner to sixty guests daily by reservation only. Lynne employs the same cooks that worked for Miss Mary, and she serves dishes prepared exactly as they have always been served. Three gardens out back provide fresh vegetables in the summertime. Other fresh produce is purchased from local farmers.

The food is legendary. Guests come from all over the world to visit the Jack Daniel Distillery and to sit at Miss Mary Bobo's Boarding House table, where a Lynchburg hostess greets each table. In a family setting visitors share stories about their hometown, how they heard about the boardinghouse and what prompted them to stop by. Southern food and hospitality have made the restaurant famous.

The Bobo Hotel, *circa* 1920

DEVILED CRACKERS

½ cup vegetable oil
1 package Original Ranch Buttermilk Dressing mix
2 teaspoons dill weed
Dash each of garlic and onion powder
1 10-ounce package oyster crackers

Combine all ingredients except crackers. Pour over crackers and stir until coated. Place in an airtight container and set aside for 24 hours before serving. Makes approximately 2 cups.

UNUSUAL CHEESE WAFERS

1 cup all-purpose flour
½ teaspoon salt
¼ teaspoon cayenne pepper
1 cup grated sharp cheddar cheese
1 stick butter, softened
½ teaspoon Worcestershire sauce
1 cup Rice Crispies cereal

Combine flour, salt and pepper. Set aside. Combine cheese, butter and Worcestershire sauce. Blend in flour mixture. Stir in cereal. Chill dough for several hours. Preheat oven to 400°. Form the dough into 1-inch balls and place on cookie sheet. Flatten with fork in a criss-cross pattern. Bake for 10 to 12 minutes or until lightly browned. Makes 3 dozen.

PARTY PECANS

2 tablespoons butter
1 cup pecan halves
2 tablespoons Jack Daniel's Whiskey
2 teaspoons soy sauce
½ teaspoon salt
2 drops hot pepper sauce

Melt butter in frying pan. Spread pecan halves in pan. Sauté very slowly, stirring often, until pecans are lightly browned. Stir in Jack Daniel's Whiskey; simmer for 1 minute. Add soy sauce, salt and hot pepper sauce. Stir. Cool pecans on paper towels. Store in airtight container. Makes 1 cup.

ARTICHOKE SQUARES

2 6-ounce jars marinated artichoke hearts
1 small onion, chopped
1 clove garlic, minced
4 eggs, beaten
¼ cup bread crumbs
¼ teaspoon red pepper sauce
½ teaspoon dried oregano
2 cups grated cheddar cheese
Salt and pepper to taste

Preheat oven to 325°. Drain liquid from one jar of artichokes into skillet. Sauté the onion and garlic in artichoke liquid until soft. Drain liquid from remaining jar of artichokes and discard. Chop all artichoke hearts. Combine eggs, bread crumbs, pepper sauce and oregano. Stir in onion mixture, artichokes, cheese, salt and pepper. Pour into greased 9x13-inch baking pan. Bake for 30 to 35 minutes. Cool. Cut into small squares. Makes 8 to 10 servings.

HERBED PUFFS

1 cup milk
5 tablespoons butter
¼ teaspoon salt
1 cup all-purpose flour
4 eggs, at room temperature
½ cup shredded Swiss cheese
¼ cup finely chopped green onions
1 teaspoon dill weed
⅛ teaspoon dry mustard

Preheat oven to 425°. In a saucepan, over medium heat, combine milk, butter and salt and bring to a boil; remove from heat. With a wooden spoon, beat in flour until dough forms a ball. Beat in eggs, one at a time, until well blended. Stir in cheese, onion, dill weed and dry mustard. Drop by teaspoonful onto a greased cookie sheet. Bake for 15 to 20 minutes until puffed and lightly brown. (They will be firm to the touch.) Makes 3 dozen.

UNFORGETTABLE HAM BALLS

        1 pound ground cooked ham
    ½ pound ground fresh pork
1½ cups soft bread crumbs (about 3 slices)
    2 tablespoons Jack Daniel's Whiskey, divided
    2 tablespoons water
    1 egg
    ¼ cup minced celery
    2 tablespoons minced onion
    ½ teaspoon dry mustard
    ¼ teaspoon pepper
    ⅛ teaspoon ground cloves
    ⅓ cup firmly packed brown sugar
    1 tablespoon prepared mustard
    ½ tablespoon vinegar

Preheat oven to 350°. Combine ham, pork, crumbs, 1 tablespoon Jack Daniel's Whiskey, water, egg, celery, onion, dry mustard, pepper and cloves. Shape mixture into meatballs (1 tablespoon each). Arrange on baking sheet; bake for 15 minutes or until fully cooked. Make sauce of brown sugar, prepared mustard, vinegar and remaining 1 tablespoon Jack Daniel's Whiskey. Stir over low heat until hot. Use toothpicks to dip cooked meatballs in sauce. Makes 20 to 25 meatballs.

PECAN CHICKEN SALAD

    1 cup finely chopped cooked chicken
    ¼ cup mayonnaise
    ¼ cup sour cream
    ¼ cup finely chopped celery
    ¼ cup toasted and finely chopped pecans
        Salt and pepper to taste

Combine all ingredients. Serve on fancy crackers. Makes 1½ cups.

CATFISH COCKTAIL

    1 pound farm-raised catfish filets, fresh or frozen
    2 cups chicken broth
    1 8-ounce bottle lime juice, chilled
    ⅓ cup thinly sliced celery
    6 tablespoons chopped onion
    2 tablespoons chopped green pepper
    1 tablespoon chopped fresh parsley
    1 cup chili sauce, chilled
    2 teaspoons prepared horseradish
        Red pepper sauce to taste
    1 avocado, peeled and diced
        Lettuce
        Parsley sprigs and lime slices

Thaw fish if frozen. Cut into 1-inch cubes. Heat broth to a boil; reduce heat and add fish. Cook for 3 to 5 minutes or until fish flakes easily with a fork. Drain well. Place in a glass bowl (anything non-metallic) and pour cold lime juice over the fish. Cover and refrigerate for 30 minutes. Combine celery, onion, pepper, parsley, chili sauce, horseradish and pepper sauce. Mix well; set aside. Drain fish. Add fish cubes and avocado to sauce mixture; toss gently. Serve on shredded lettuce. Garnish with parsley sprigs and lime slices. This may be prepared ahead and refrigerated. Makes 6 appetizers.

TUNA AND SHRIMP PATÉ

1 10-ounce can tuna, drained
1 cup (2 sticks) butter, softened
2 to 3 drops lemon juice
2 to 3 drops hot pepper sauce
Salt
Pepper
10 medium shrimp, cooked and shelled
3 tablespoons chopped pimientos
2 tablespoons capers, drained
Parsley

Using a food processor with metal blade, combine tuna, butter, lemon juice, pepper sauce, and salt and pepper to taste. Process until mixture is smooth. Add shrimp, pimiento and capers. Process until ingredients are evenly chopped and combined. Taste and adjust seasoning (must be highly seasoned). Pour into well-oiled 3-cup loaf pan or mold. Chill 24 hours. Unmold and garnish with parsley. Serve with toast rounds or crackers. Makes 3 cups.

FISH PATÉ

4 tablespoons unsalted butter, at room temperature
1½ cups cold cooked fish, skin & bones removed
1 tablespoon lemon juice
1 tablespoon finely chopped chives
1 tablespoon finely chopped dill weed
Salt
Freshly ground pepper

Using food processor: Process all ingredients with steel blade until well combined. *By hand:* Cream butter until very soft. Mash fish well; blend into butter. Add the lemon juice and seasonings; mix well. Pack into a small bowl or crock; chill at least 6 hours or overnight. Serve on toast or crackers. Makes 1½ cups.

SPINACH TARTS

1 3-ounce package cream cheese, softened
½ cup butter (1 stick), softened
1½ cups all-purpose flour
1 10-ounce package frozen spinach, thawed
1 egg, beaten
¼ teaspoon salt
⅛ teaspoon pepper
2 tablespoons minced onion
1 cup grated Romano cheese
4 tablespoons butter, melted
Pimiento strips

Preheat oven to 350°. Combine first 3 ingredients. Using one tablespoon of dough each, press into ungreased miniature muffin pans to form tiny shells. Drain spinach and squeeze to remove all moisture. Chop spinach very fine. Combine all remaining ingredients, except pimiento. Spoon into unbaked tart shells. Bake for 30 to 35 minutes. Garnish each with small piece of pimiento. Makes 2½ dozen.

MULBERRY CREEK RUMAKI

½ pound chicken livers
½ pound bacon
1 small can whole water chestnuts, drained
¼ cup Jack Daniel's Whiskey
¼ cup soy sauce
3 tablespoons honey

Preheat oven to 400°. Separate livers. Cut bacon slices in half. Cut chestnuts in half. Combine Jack Daniel's Whiskey, soy sauce and honey. Dip livers in mixture and coat well. Wrap bacon around a piece of liver and a chestnut half; secure with toothpick. Place on rack atop baking sheet. Bake for 20 minutes or until bacon is crisp, turning once. Makes 24 to 30 servings.

Steak Tartare

2 eggs, beaten
2 tablespoons grated onion
1 teaspoon Worcestershire sauce
¼ cup Jack Daniel's Whiskey
1 pound fresh lean sirloin, ground
1 teaspoon pepper
1 teaspoon salt
2 teaspoons finely chopped fresh parsley
¼ cup finely chopped fresh mushrooms

Combine eggs, onion, Worcestershire sauce and Jack Daniel's Whiskey. Add to sirloin; gently mix with two forks. Sprinkle pepper, salt, parsley and mushrooms over meat; mix lightly until all ingredients are blended. Careful blending is important to attain the desired light, almost fluffy texture. Rough mixing makes it too heavy. Serve with dark bread. Makes 24 to 30 servings.

Poor Man's Caviar

1 large eggplant
2 tablespoons vegetable oil
1 small onion, finely chopped
1 clove garlic, minced
¼ cup finely chopped green pepper
1½ tablespoons lemon juice
1 teaspoon salt
   Freshly ground pepper

Preheat broiler. Slice eggplant into halves. Oil flat surfaces and place halves flat-side down on a baking sheet. Broil 3 inches from heat for 20 to 25 minutes or until quite soft. Discard skin and mash pulp. Sauté onion, garlic and green pepper in remaining oil until tender. Add lemon juice, and salt and pepper to taste. Combine eggplant with onion mixture. Chill 2 to 3 hours before serving. Serve with crackers. Makes 2 cups.

Uncle Jack's Red Dogs

1½ cups catsup
¼ cup brown sugar
¼ cup Jack Daniel's Whiskey
1 package cocktail wieners or hot dogs cut into 1-inch pieces

Combine catsup and brown sugar; heat over low heat until sugar dissolves. Remove from heat and add Jack Daniel's Whiskey. This can be served in a chafing dish with cocktail wieners or used as a sauce over hot dogs in buns. All proportions are approximate. Adjust to your own taste. Makes 24 to 30 servings.

Country Ham 'n Cheese Balls

½ cup butter, softened
1½ cups shredded cheddar cheese
¼ cup finely chopped country ham
¼ teaspoon Worcestershire sauce
Dash of hot pepper sauce
1 cup all-purpose flour

Preheat oven to 350°. Mix butter, cheese, ham and seasonings well. Add flour and blend well. Pinch dough off and roll into 1-inch diameter balls. Place on cookie sheet. Bake for 15 minutes. Serve hot. Makes approximately 3 to 4 dozen.

Pineapple à la Jack Daniel

½ cup sugar
½ cup water
½ cup Jack Daniel's Whiskey
2 fresh pineapples, cut into cubes

Bring sugar and water to a boil; simmer for a few minutes. Remove from heat. Add Jack Daniel's Whiskey. Pour over pineapple cubes and chill for a few hours in refrigerator. This makes the pineapple taste fruitier and sweeter than using a sugary liqueur. Accompany with a few simple cookies and coffee. Delicious! Makes approximately 2 cups.

Stuffed Mushrooms

20 medium mushrooms
½ cup butter, softened
2 tablespoons finely chopped green onion
1 teaspoon finely chopped parsley
¼ cup Fontina cheese, grated
Salt to taste
1 cup heavy cream

Preheat oven to 425°. Brush off mushrooms (or wipe with paper towel) to clean. Remove stems and scoop out small amount of pulp from centers of mushrooms. Chop stems and pulp. Combine with butter, onion, parsley and cheese. Sprinkle mushroom caps with salt. Stuff with filling; mound up on top. Place mushrooms into a greased baking dish. Pour cream in bottom. Bake for 15 minutes. Remove mushrooms from the cream; keep warm. Pour cream into saucepan; heat until reduced by half. Spoon over mushrooms. Serve warm. Makes 20 mushrooms.

SOUPS & SALADS

BLACK-EYED PEA SOUP

1 pound dried black-eyed peas
4 slices bacon
1 onion, chopped
Vegetable oil
1 tablespoon all-purpose flour
2 quarts water
2 tomatoes, chopped
2 cloves garlic, minced
1 teaspoon Worcestershire sauce
1 teaspoon dried red pepper flakes
Salt and pepper to taste
1 cup cooked rice

Wash and sort peas removing any that float or are discolored. Cover peas with cold water; bring to a boil and simmer for 2 minutes. Remove from heat and set aside, tightly covered, for 1 hour. Drain peas and set aside. Fry bacon in Dutch oven until crisp; remove bacon and set aside. Sauté onion in bacon drippings until tender. Add enough oil to drippings to make two tablespoons. Stir in flour and cook for several minutes. Add bacon, peas, water, tomatoes and seasonings. Cook over low heat about 2½ hours or until peas are tender. Garnish individual bowls with a small scoop of rice floating atop soup. Makes 6 to 8 servings.

BUTTERMILK CUCUMBER SOUP

2 medium cucumbers or 1 large cucumber
2 cups buttermilk
2 cups chicken stock (homemade is best)
2 teaspoons salt
Freshly ground pepper
2 tablespoons chopped chives
Chopped dill weed

Peel cucumbers and remove the seeds. Shred cucumbers in a food processor or with a grater. Mix the cucumbers in a bowl with the buttermilk and chicken stock. Add salt, pepper and chives. Refrigerate the soup for several hours before serving. Garnish with chopped dill weed. Makes 4 to 6 servings.

CATFISH SOUP

6 slices bacon
1 onion, chopped
4 catfish, skinned, heads and tails removed, and cut
    into pieces
2 cups water
1 tablespoon parsley, finely chopped
    Salt and pepper to taste
1 tablespoon butter
2 tablespoons all-purpose flour
1 cup heavy cream
3 egg yolks

Fry bacon in Dutch oven until crisp. Remove bacon and crumble; set aside. Sauté onion in bacon drippings until tender. Add fish and pour in water. Add parsley, salt and pepper; bring to a boil. Simmer for 15 minutes or until fish is tender and flakes easily with a fork. Remove fish from stock and de-bone. Set aside. Reserve stock. Melt butter in saucepan; blend in flour. Slowly stir in cream. Add small amount of the hot cream to the beaten yolks, add yolks to cream. Stir into the fish stock. Cook over low heat until thickened. Add fish. Adjust seasoning. Garnish with crumbled bacon. Makes 4 servings.

CHICKEN AND MUSHROOM CHOWDER

2 tablespoons vegetable oil
4 cups sliced fresh mushrooms
½ cup chopped onion
½ cup sliced celery
2 cups chicken broth
1 16-ounce can tomatoes, undrained and chopped
2 tablespoons rice, uncooked
    Salt and pepper to taste
1 bay leaf
2 cups cubed cooked chicken
3 tablespoons dry sherry
    French bread

Heat oil in large pot; sauté mushrooms, onion and celery until tender. Add broth, tomatoes, rice, salt, pepper and bay leaf. Simmer, covered, until rice is tender, about 30 minutes. Add chicken and heat thoroughly. Remove bay leaf. Add ½ tablespoon sherry to each bowl of soup. Serve with toasted French bread. Makes 6 servings.

CORN CHOWDER

3 tablespoons butter
1 medium onion, chopped
4 cups fresh corn kernels or 2 10-ounce packages
    frozen corn, thawed
⅓ cup Jack Daniel's Whiskey
3 tablespoons all-purpose flour
2 cups chicken stock
2 cups cream
    Salt and cayenne pepper to taste
2 potatoes, peeled, cut into cubes and cooked

Melt butter in a large saucepan over medium heat. Add onion; sauté 5 minutes. Add corn; continue to cook until corn is slightly soft. Pour in Jack Daniel's Whiskey and carefully ignite. Tilt pot so flame touches all the corn. When flame goes out, stir in flour. Slowly stir in the stock, cream, salt and cayenne pepper. Heat until thickened. Add potato cubes. Heat through; serve hot. Makes 6 to 8 servings.

HAM AND CHEESE CHOWDER

2 cups peeled and cubed potatoes
3 tablespoons butter
1 cup chopped onion
½ cup finely chopped carrots
3 tablespoons all-purpose flour
3 cups milk
1½ cups diced cooked ham
1½ cups grated cheddar cheese
    Salt and pepper to taste
    Croutons

Cook potatoes in lightly salted water until tender; reserve cooking liquid. Melt butter in large pot; sauté onion and carrots until tender. Blend in flour. Stir in milk and 1 cup potato liquid. Cook, stirring constantly, until mixture is smooth and thickened. Add ham, potatoes and cheese; stir until cheese is melted. Season with salt and pepper. Garnish top with croutons. Makes 8 servings.

HOT WEATHER HERBED TOMATO SOUP

4½ cups chopped tomatoes
2 cups chopped onion
¼ cup vegetable oil
1 tablespoon tomato paste
1½ teaspoons salt
2 cloves garlic, minced

1 tablespoon cornstarch
1 teaspoon sugar
2 cups water, divided
3 cups chicken stock
⅓ cup lightly packed fresh basil leaves
Salt and white pepper to taste
¼ cup olive oil
Basil leaves

Combine first six ingredients in heavy saucepan over low heat. Simmer for 25 minutes, stirring often. Combine cornstarch and sugar; gradually stir in ½ cup water. Set aside. Add remaining water, chicken stock and basil leaves to tomato mixture. When mixture is hot, but not boiling, slowly stir in cornstarch liquid. Simmer until thickened. Remove from heat. Using steel blades in food processor, purée soup in several small batches. Adjust to taste with salt and pepper. Chill 4 to 5 hours. Before serving whisk in olive oil. Garnish with small basil leaves. Makes about 2½ quarts.

JACK'S BLACK BEAN SOUP

1 10-ounce can black bean soup
1 cup water
1 teaspoon beef bouillon powder or 1 cube
3 tablespoons Jack Daniel's Whiskey
   Hard-boiled eggs

Combine first 4 ingredients and simmer over low heat for 10 minutes. Garnish with thin slices of hard-boiled eggs. Makes 2 servings.

MELON SOUP

4 cups cantaloupe chunks (or honeydew melon)
1½ cups orange juice
¼ cup lime juice
2 tablespoons honey
1½ cups sweet sparkling white wine, chilled

In a food processor fitted with steel blade, purée melon in small batches until smooth. Combine melon purée with orange juice, lime juice and honey. Chill. Add sparkling wine before serving. This is refreshing served at an outdoor barbecue. Makes 6 servings.

OYSTERS ROCKEFELLER SOUP

1½ cups chicken broth, divided
1 small onion, finely chopped
1 stalk celery, finely chopped
2 cloves garlic, minced
1 cup finely chopped fresh spinach
1 pint shucked oysters
⅓ cup Parmesan cheese
2 cups half-and-half
2 tablespoons cornstarch
1½ teaspoons anise seed
½ teaspoon salt
⅛ teaspoon ground pepper

In large pan, combine ½ cup broth, onion, celery and garlic; cover and cook for 5 minutes. Add chopped spinach; simmer 5 minutes longer. Drain oysters; add liquid to broth in pan. Continue to simmer, stirring occasionally. Stir in cheese. Combine half-and-half, cornstarch and seasonings. Slowly stir into simmering soup. Stirring constantly, simmer until thick and bubbly. Stir in oysters and heat through. Serve immediately. Makes 6 servings.

PEASANT SOUP

6 cups beef broth
1 cup dry red wine
¼ pound bacon, chopped
1½ cups cooked navy beans
2 cups shredded cabbage
1 cup diced potatoes
1 cup diced carrots
1 cup diced celery
1 cup chopped onion
1 clove garlic, minced
1 16-ounce can tomatoes, undrained and chopped
Salt and pepper to taste
1 cup macaroni, uncooked
Grated Parmesan cheese

Combine all ingredients, except macaroni and cheese, in a heavy soup kettle. Bring to a boil; lower heat, simmer about 40 minutes. Add macaroni and cook until macaroni is tender. Garnish each bowl of soup with grated cheese. This is good served with cornbread wedges. Makes 8 to 10 servings.

PREMIUM ONION SOUP

2 cups thinly sliced yellow onions
3 tablespoons butter
8 cups beef broth
Pinch of powdered thyme
¼ cup Jack Daniel's Whiskey
Salt and pepper
6 thickly sliced pieces of French bread, toasted
½ cup grated Parmesan cheese
½ cup grated Gruyère cheese

Sauté onion in butter in Dutch oven until lightly browned. Add broth, thyme and Jack Daniel's Whiskey; simmer for 35 to 40 minutes. Salt and pepper to taste. Pour into individual oven-proof dishes. Top each with a slice of toast and a sprinkle of both cheeses. Broil until cheese is melted and lightly browned. Makes 8 servings.

VICHYSQUASH SOUP

2 medium onions, chopped
3 tablespoons butter
3 cups sliced yellow crookneck squash
1 cup chicken stock
Salt and white pepper to taste
1½ cups half-and-half
½ cup sour cream
Chopped fresh chives

Cook onion in butter in large saucepan over medium heat until transparent. Add squash and chicken stock. Cover and cook until vegetables are tender. Cool. Purée in food processor in small batches. Season with salt and pepper. Chill. Before serving, blend in half-and-half and sour cream. Garnish with chopped chives. Makes 6 servings.

The Cave Spring

. . . .

The hills of Tennessee are dotted liberally with springs producing iron-free water, making this a natural region for making good whiskey. In 1866, Jack Daniel registered his distillery here in a Tennessee hollow, next to a beautiful cave spring. The water from the cave spring was iron-free limestone water that flowed at a constant 56°, no matter what the weather. It was cool enough to cool the still and pure enough to water the proof.

Since that historic day, the United States' oldest registered distillery has continued to produce Tennessee Sour Mash Whiskey, with the exception of the time of prohibition.

In 1904, Mr. Jack Daniel took samples of his fine produce to the St. Louis World's Fair. He entered it in the whiskey judging competition and walked away with a gold medal for the world's finest whiskey. This was the first time that the world at large was introduced to Jack Daniel's Tennessee Sour Mash Sipping Whiskey. Who was to know what a historic moment this was. Mr. Jack died in 1911 and left his whiskey operation to his nephew, Lem Motlow.

Although Jack Daniel's Whiskey is now marketed all over the world, it is right here in this Tennessee hollow that all of the whiskey is made—because good water makes good whiskey.

West Texas Pinto Bean Soup

1⅓ cups pinto beans
8 cups chicken stock
½ pound bacon, chopped
1 clove garlic, minced
½ cup chopped onion
2 teaspoons chili powder
⅓ cup chopped green chile peppers
Salt
½ cup diced cooked ham

Soak pinto beans in water overnight. Drain and place in a Dutch oven. Add stock and bring to a boil. Lower heat and simmer for 1 hour. Add remaining ingredients, except salt and ham. Simmer for another hour. Add salt and simmer 1 hour longer. Remove ⅓ of beans and liquid and mash together (easily done in a food processor). Return to pot. Heat thoroughly. Adjust seasoning. Garnish soup with diced ham to serve. Makes 6 to 8 servings.

Farmhouse Cole Slaw

1 head of cabbage, finely chopped
1 small onion, chopped
1 green pepper, chopped
1 cup raisins
1½ cups vegetable oil
1 cup sugar
½ cup white apple cider vinegar
½ teaspoon celery seed
½ teaspoon salt

Combine first 4 ingredients; set aside. Place remaining ingredients in blender; blend well. Add dressing to chopped slaw, tossing well to cover. Chill. Toss again before serving. May be topped with slivered almonds, if desired. Makes 6 to 8 servings.

Whipped Cream Cole Slaw

1 cup apple cider vinegar
1 cup sugar
Salt and pepper
1 head cabbage, chopped or grated
1 cup whipping cream
1 teaspoon prepared mustard
2 tablespoons salad dressing
1 tablespoon sugar

Mix vinegar with sugar. Add salt and pepper to taste. Cover cabbage with vinegar mixture. Top with 6 to 10 ice cubes. Chill for about 6 hours. Whip cream; add remaining ingredients as cream whips to form soft peaks. Completely drain cabbage of vinegar. Add whipped dressing and serve. Makes 6 servings.

Charcoal Mellowing

· ·

Tennessee whiskey is different from other whiskeys. In neighboring states like Kentucky, distilleries make bourbon, which is similar to Tennessee whiskey because both are made from a grain mash fermentation, but only Tennessee whiskey is charcoal mellowed. It is this process that makes it different and gives it a unique taste.

Hard sugar maple trees are grown high on the hillsides. Farmers cut these trees and bring them to the Jack Daniel Distillery. Logs are split and cut into four-foot pieces and stacked into four-foot ricks at the rickyard. These ricks are then burned out in the open.

When the rick is burned a large pile of charcoal remains, which is pulverized into pea-sized pieces. The charcoal is used to fill 12-foot deep vats in the mellowing house. Here the whiskey trickles over the charcoal slowly, drop by drop, to filter, leach or mellow the whiskey. This one process removes the grain taste and only a smooth, distinctively different taste remains.

It is Jack Daniel's Tennessee Sour Mash Sipping Whiskey that is the Spirit of Tennessee.

OLD-FASHIONED COLE SLAW
(Circa 1870)

Some recipes have been around so long that they deserve a certain amount of respect just for their endurance. Other recipes, however deserve repeating because one of us might have missed them and they are too good to lose. Such is the case with this recipe, dated 1870, and shared by Marthella Sanders. If cole slaw can be called delectable, then this recipe would top the list.

1½ pounds cabbage, sliced and chopped
1 teaspoon salt
⅔ cup sugar
⅓ cup vinegar
1 cup heavy cream, whipped

Place cabbage in a covered bowl in refrigerator for several hours. Combine remaining ingredients; cover and place in refrigerator. Mix cabbage and dressing 30 minutes before serving; chill. Makes 6 to 8 servings.

COLD BEEF SALAD

2 cups rare roast beef, chilled
½ cup thinly sliced celery
⅓ cup chopped sour pickle
¼ cup chopped green onion
¼ cup capers, drained
3 tablespoons vinegar
1 tablespoon Dijon-style mustard
½ clove garlic, minced
½ teaspoon parsley
Dash of cayenne pepper
½ cup vegetable oil

Toss first 5 ingredients together. Whisk together remaining ingredients and pour over beef mixture. Serve at room temperature. Makes 4 servings.

POTATO SALAD

4 cups cubed cooked potatoes
1 tablespoon grated onion
2 hard-boiled eggs, chopped
½ cup chopped celery
1 tablespoon minced parsley
¼ cup cubed American cheese
¼ cup chopped green pepper
¼ cup sour cream
½ cup mayonnaise
Salt and pepper to taste

Combine all ingredients in large bowl. Chill. May be garnished with tomato wedges. Makes 6 cups.

CONGEALED ASPARAGUS SALAD

1 cup sugar
1 cup water
½ cup vinegar
2½ envelopes unflavored gelatin
½ cup cold water
½ cup lemon juice
2 10½-ounce cans asparagus tips, drained and liquid reserved
1 cup diced celery
1 2-ounce can chopped pimientos, drained
1 teaspoon grated onion
½ cup chopped pecans
Mayonnaise
Pimiento strips

Bring sugar, water and vinegar to a boil; add gelatin that has been dissolved in ½ cup cold water, lemon juice and 1 cup reserved asparagus liquid. Refrigerate until partially congealed; fold in next 4 ingredients and asparagus. Pour into 6-cup mold that has been rinsed with cold water. Chill overnight or until set. Cut into squares. Serve with mayonnaise topped with pimiento strips. Makes 8 to 10 servings.

Barrels and Barrelhouses
. . . .

Above the Jack Daniel hollow in Lynchburg, the hills are dotted with gray square buildings that immediately notify any visitor that he is in whiskey making country. After the sour mash is cooked and distilled in the hollow, the whiskey—as clear as pure water—is placed in charred white oak barrels to age. Once in the barrels the whiskey is placed in warehouses where the heat causes the wood of the barrels to expand and the whiskey works its way into the charred oak. When the air blows cool at night high in the hills and the wood contracts, it pushes the whiskey back into the barrel. It is this motion in-and-out of the wood of the barrel that ages and colors the whiskey. Good whiskey ages in about four years. When the barrel is opened, the liquid has become a rich caramel color.

In the days of prohibition when illegal stills were running wild, their moonshine was called "white lightning." It was "white" because the whiskey was never allowed to age and thus never acquired the characteristic brown color from the charred wood. It was called "lightning" because of the proof or purity of the whiskey. In these parts, lightning is more than mere humans can handle!

Barrel trucks deliver barrels filled with whiskey to be aged to the barrelhouses and return with barrels filled with aged whiskey to be bottled. All during this process, the whiskey is carefully monitored by the federal government. Only when it is bottled and has a tax stamp affixed verifying that all taxes have been paid is the whiskey legal for sale.

The empty barrels, meanwhile, are discarded. Good whiskey comes from aging in new charred oak barrels. Other products like brandy, cognac, wine or Scotch whiskey can age in old barrels, but Jack Daniel's ages only in new barrels.

Around these parts you see a lot of barrel furniture, barrel flower planters and even some barrels that are used to catch rainwater. If you look real close when the weather gets a little cool you will see a slight golden color in the clear rainwater.

KRAUT SALAD

2½ cups chopped kraut, drained
½ cup chopped celery
½ cup chopped green peppers
½ cup chopped onion
2 tablespoons chopped pimientos
1 cup sugar
1 cup vinegar
¼ cup vegetable oil
Salt and pepper to taste

Combine all ingredients in the order given and mix well. Chill. Salad will keep for weeks. Makes 8 to 10 servings.

FAUCON SALAD

Some years ago in downtown Nashville there was a restaurant named Faucon's, and the salad that they served was prized by one and all. After the restaurant closed the recipe was printed in The Tennessean for all of those who requested it and felt that more than a restaurant had been lost to time. The salad, appropriately called *Faucon Salad,* is still served locally at a couple of other restaurants and is as popular today as it was then.

Garlic clove
Lettuce
Roquefort cheese
1 hard-boiled egg per serving
Olive oil
1 lemon, cut in half
Salt

In a large salad bowl, bruise a pod of fresh garlic against the sides and bottom of bowl. Press firmly to cover the interior; discard garlic. Break a head of lettuce that is dry and crisp into the bowl. With your hands gently and thoroughly turn the lettuce. Remove most of the lettuce to a side bowl, leaving a layer on the bottom of the bowl. Over this, crumble a generous amount of Roquefort cheese. Mince one egg on top of the cheese. Then drop on not more than three or four drops of olive oil and the merest dash of salt. Squeeze three or four drops of lemon juice. Put in another not-too-thick layer of lettuce and repeat the crumbled cheese, minced egg, and drops of oil and lemon juice. Complete the layers until you have the amount of servings you wish. Be sparse with the oil. You do not wish to drown the salad or make it even *wet.*

The Secret: The final step and secret to success, you must turn the whole thing with your hands. Turn it very gently so as not to bruise the lettuce. The French say that most Americans fatigue the lettuce when they make a salad, so gently, with the hands, turn until thoroughly mixed and the lettuce starts to take on a yellow hue from the yellow of the egg. If there is too much oil it will not do this, so it is better to have too little oil than too much. Dish into individual salad bowls and serve.

DRESSING FOR FRESH TOMATO SLICES

    1 cup mayonnaise
    1 clove garlic, minced
    1 teaspoon Worcestershire sauce
    1 tablespoon minced green onion
    ½ teaspoon dry mustard
    ½ teaspoon sugar
    ½ cup beef broth
       Salt and pepper

Combine mayonnaise, garlic, Worcestershire sauce, onion, mustard and sugar. With whisk, slowly blend in broth. Salt and pepper to taste. Refrigerate until ready to use. Delicious over fresh tomato slices or other salads. Makes 1½ cups.

FRESH TOMATO HASH

    4 medium tomatoes (3 cups) chopped and drained
    ½ cup chopped celery
    ¼ cup chopped green pepper
    1 small onion, thinly sliced
    2 tablespoons mustard seed
    2 teaspoons salt
  1½ teaspoons ground nutmeg
    ½ teaspoon ground cinnamon
    ¼ teaspoon ground cloves
    ⅓ cup vinegar

Combine first 4 ingredients; set aside. Blend remaining ingredients well. Pour dressing over vegetables; toss lightly. cover and chill a few hours. Makes 3 cups.

PEA-PICKLED SALAD

    2 16-ounce cans black-eyed peas, drained and washed
    1 onion, thinly sliced
    ½ cup olive oil
    ¼ cup apple cider vinegar
    2 cloves of garlic, crushed
    1 tablespoon Worcestershire sauce
    1 teaspoon salt
    1 bay leaf
       Pepper to taste

Combine peas and onion in heatproof bowl. Combine remaining ingredients in a saucepan and bring to a boil. Pour over peas and onions. Refrigerate overnight. Remove bay leaf. Makes 4½ cups.

Mexican Tomato Salad

2 ripe avocados
  Salt and pepper
2 tablespoons lemon juice
2 tablespoons vegetable oil
1 teaspoon balsamic vinegar
½ cup finely chopped cooked ham
  Hot pepper sauce
  Lettuce leaves
4 medium tomatoes, sliced

Halve the avocados and remove the pulp from the shell. Mash the pulp with the salt, pepper, lemon juice, oil and vinegar. Add chopped ham and hot pepper sauce to taste. Arrange lettuce on a serving plate and top with slices of tomatoes arranged in a circle. Fill the center with the avocado mixture. Makes 4 servings.

Summer Salad

3 medium cucumbers, peeled and seeded and cut into chunks
1 large sweet red onion, cut into chunks
3 large green or red peppers, seeded and cut into chunks
2 or 3 large ripe tomatoes, cut into chunks
½ cup vegetable oil
½ cup wine vinegar
  Salt and freshly ground pepper to taste

Combine all ingredients and refrigerate for 1 hour before serving. Toss several times during refrigeration. Makes 6 servings.

Early Spring Wilted Lettuce Salad

2 bunches of leaf lettuce
8 green onions, finely chopped
8 radishes, thinly sliced

6 slices bacon
¼ cup vinegar
1 tablespoon sugar
¼ teaspoon salt
¼ teaspoon pepper
2 hard-boiled eggs, finely chopped

Wash and drain leaf lettuce. Shred lettuce with a knife and place in serving bowl with onion and radishes. Cook bacon in skillet until crisp. Remove bacon and crumble. Discard all but ¼ cup bacon drippings in skillet. Add vinegar, sugar, salt and pepper and simmer until sugar is dissolved. Pour hot dressing over salad; toss. Garnish with crumbled bacon and chopped eggs. Serve immediately. Makes 6 servings.

*

Moore County Toast

**MAY THE SUN SHINE WARM UPON
YOUR FACE
AND THE RAINS FALL SOFT UPON
YOUR FIELDS.**

*

GRATED CARROT AND RAISIN SALAD

½ cup raisins
1 cup hot water
2 pounds carrots, grated
½ cup flaked coconut
½ cup drained crushed pineapple
1 cup mayonnaise

Soak raisins in hot water for 15 minutes; drain. Combine raisins, carrots, coconut and pineapple. Fold in mayonnaise; chill before serving. Makes 8 to 10 servings.

ROQUEFORT WALNUT SALAD

1 head romaine lettuce, rinsed
5 tablespoons olive oil
1 tablespoon red wine vinegar
½ teaspoon salt
⅛ teaspoon pepper
¼ pound Roquefort cheese or bleu cheese
½ cup chopped English walnuts

Dry lettuce and tear into bite-sized pieces; set aside. Place the oil, vinegar, salt and pepper into a salad bowl. Beat with a fork until well combined. Add half the cheese and mash into the oil mixture. Add half the nuts; toss mixture with lettuce. Top salad with remaining cheese and nuts. Makes 6 to 8 servings.

SUNDAY FRUIT SALAD

4 eggs, beaten
4 tablespoons vinegar
4 tablespoons sugar
2 tablespoons butter, melted
2 cups Bing cherries, drained
2 cups pineapple chunks, drained
2 cups cubed orange sections
2 cups miniature marshmallows
1 cup heavy cream, whipped

Combine eggs, vinegar, sugar, and butter in double boiler over simmering water. Cook and stir until smooth. Remove from heat; set aside to cool. When cooled, fold in fruit, marshmallows and whipped cream. Pour into pan and chill for 24 hours. Makes 8 to 10 servings.

SPIKED CHERRY SALAD

1½ cups boiling water
1 6-ounce package black cherry gelatin
¾ cup juice from drained cherries
¼ cup Jack Daniel's Whiskey
1 16-ounce can tart red cherries, drained
3 tablespoons lemon juice
1 cup miniature marshmallows
½ cup chopped pecans
Lettuce leaves

Pour boiling water over gelatin; stir until dissolved. Add cherry juice, Jack Daniel's Whiskey and lemon juice. Chill until nearly set. Blend in cherries, marshmallows and pecans. Place salad in a mold that has been rinsed with cold water. When firm, cut into squares and serve on lettuce leaves. Makes 8 servings.

Tomato Cream Mold

1 pound fresh ripe tomatoes, peeled and cored
1 envelope unflavored gelatin
   Salt
   Sugar
1 cup heavy cream, whipped
   Watercress or flat-leaved parsley

Purée the tomatoes in a food processor; this should produce 2 cups of purée. Sprinkle gelatin over ¼ cup of the puree and bring the rest of the puree to a boil in a small saucepan. Season the tomatoes with a little salt and sugar; simmer for several minutes. Add the softened gelatin and stir very thoroughly to be sure it is well dissolved. Cool the tomatoes to room temperature. *Do not* refrigerate or the gelatin will set. Blend the cooled tomatoes thoroughly with the whipped cream. Adjust seasonings, adding sugar or salt as needed. Pour the tomato cream into a 1-quart mold or individual molds that have been rinsed with cold water; chill until set. Unmold and garnish with watercress or flat-leaved parsley. This has a light, rich, intense tomato taste. It is delicious with cold, poached fish. Makes 6 servings.

Note: Don't attempt to make this out of season. Only very fresh summer tomatoes produce a good mold.

Zippy Cider Salad

1 tablespoon unflavored gelatin
1¾ cups apple cider
2 tablespoons sugar
1 tablespoon lemon juice
¼ cup Jack Daniel's Whiskey
2 cups unpeeled and grated apples
½ cup raisins
   Lettuce leaves

In a saucepan, sprinkle gelatin over apple cider to soften. Add sugar and lemon juice and Jack Daniel's Whiskey; stir over low heat until gelatin dissolves. Chill until slightly set; fold in apples and raisins. Pour mixture into oiled mold. Chill until firm. Unmold onto lettuce leaves. Makes 8 servings.

MOLDED AVOCADO SALAD

  2 small avocados, peeled and mashed
  ¼ cup lemon juice
  2 tablespoons unflavored gelatin
  1 cup chicken broth, divided
  1 cup sour cream
  ½ cup mayonnaise
  ¼ teaspoon celery salt
    Hot pepper sauce to taste
    Lettuce leaves
    Cherry tomatoes

In food processor, purée avocado with half the lemon juice. Soak gelatin in ½ cup chicken broth; dissolve over low heat. Add remaining broth and lemon juice and set aside to cool. Combine next 4 ingredients with avocado mixture and gelatin mixture. Pour into oiled 4-cup ring mold. Chill until firm. Unmold onto bed of lettuce leaves. Fill center with cherry tomatoes. This is delicious served with bleu cheese dressing. Makes 6 to 8 servings.

PINK CRABMEAT SALAD MOLD

  1 10½-ounce can tomato soup
  4 3-ounce packages cream cheese, softened
  3 tablespoons unflavored gelatin
  1 cup water
  1 cup mayonnaise
  2 tablespoons grated onion
  1 cup finely chopped celery
  1 teaspoon lemon juice
  1 teaspoon finely chopped parsley
  ½ teaspoon hot pepper sauce
  3 cups white crabmeat, shredded, shell and cartilage removed
    Parsley sprigs

In a food processor, combine soup and cream cheese until smooth. Sprinkle gelatin over water in a saucepan; soften for 1 minute then heat to dissolve. Set aside to cool. To soup mixture, add mayonnaise, onion, celery, lemon juice, parsley and hot pepper sauce. Remove from processor and whisk in cooled gelatin mixture. Fold in crabmeat and pour into a mold that has been rinsed with cold water. Chill until set. Unmold and garnish with sprigs of parsley. Makes 6 to 8 servings.

Left: *Circa 1890*. The first bar to ever serve Jack Daniel's Old No. 7 Whiskey was the White Rabbit Saloon in Lynchburg.
Right: The White Rabbit Saloon today

PINEAPPLE-MARSHMALLOW SALAD

This salad must be made a day before serving time.

1 tablespoon all-purpose flour
½ teaspoon salt
1 tablespoon sugar
3 egg yolks, beaten
3 tablespoons vinegar
1 tablespoon butter
1½ cups milk
1 16-ounce can crushed pineapple, drained
1½ cups miniature marshmallows
1 cup chopped pecans
1 cup heavy cream, whipped

Combine flour, salt and sugar; add egg yolks, vinegar, butter and milk. Simmer, stirring constantly, until mixture thickens; remove from heat and cool. Fold in remaining ingredients. Store in covered container in refrigerator for 24 hours before serving. Makes 8 to 10 servings.

WHISKEY SOUR SALAD

2 tablespoons unflavored gelatin
¼ cup cold water
¾ cup boiling water
½ cup sugar
1½ cups orange juice
Juice of two lemons

½ cup Jack Daniel's Whiskey
1 8-ounce can crushed pineapple, well drained
½ cup chopped pecans
1 cup miniature marshmallows
   Whipped cream
   Maraschino cherries

Soften gelatin in cold water for several minutes. Stir into boiling water. Lower heat. Add sugar and stir until dissolved. Cool. Add orange juice, lemon juice and Jack Daniel's Whiskey. Chill in refrigerator until partially set. Fold in pineapple, pecans and marshmallows. Chill until firm. To serve, cut into squares; garnish with whipped cream and maraschino cherries. Makes 12 servings.

HONEYDEW AND GREEN GRAPE SALAD

½ medium honeydew melon, seeded and peeled
   Lettuce leaves
1½ cups halved seedless green grapes
¼ cup vegetable oil
2 tablespoons lime juice
¼ teaspoon sugar
¼ teaspoon salt
   Freshly ground pepper to taste

Cut melon into thin slices and divide slices between 4 salad plates covered with lettuce leaves. Sprinkle the grapes evenly over the melon slices. Whisk together remaining ingredients and spoon over fruit. Makes 4 servings.

FROZEN TOMATO SALAD WITH HORSERADISH DRESSING

2 1-pound cans tomatoes, well drained
1 cup mayonnaise

⅓ cup sour cream
2 tablespoons lemon juice
1 tablespoon finely chopped green onion
1 teaspoon Worcestershire sauce
⅛ teaspoon red pepper sauce
1 teaspoon salt
1 tablespoon unflavored gelatin, softened in ⅓ cup water

Dressing:
1 cup mayonnaise
½ cup sour cream
¼ teaspoon dry mustard
4 teaspoons prepared horseradish
2 cloves garlic, minced
   Chives for garnish

Combine first 9 ingredients in food processor and process until well blended. Pour into container; cover and place in freezer. Stir several times as it freezes. When frozen, scoop out with ice cream scoop. Whisk next 5 ingredients together. Refrigerate until serving time. Spoon over scoops of frozen tomato salad; garnish with chives. Makes 6 to 8 servings.

MOLDED BEET SALAD

1 1-pound can diced beets (reserve liquid)
2 3-ounce packages lemon-flavored gelatin
⅓ cup sugar
⅓ cup vinegar
1½ tablespoons mustard seed
⅛ teaspoon salt
1 cup cold water
1 cup chopped celery
½ cup grated onion
    Lettuce leaves

Drain beets. Measure beet liquid and add water to make 2⅓ cups. Heat to a boil and stir in gelatin until dissolved. Add sugar, vinegar, mustard seed and salt. Remove from heat. Add cold water. Chill until partially set. Fold in beets, celery and onion. Pour into a 1½-quart mold that has been rinsed with water. Chill several hours or until firm. Unmold onto lettuce leaves. Makes 8 to 10 servings.

SUPREME CRANBERRY SALAD

1 large box cherry-flavored gelatin
2 cups boiling water
1 16-ounce can whole cranberry sauce
1 16-ounce can whole purple plums
½ cup chopped pecans

Dissolve gelatin in boiling water. Add whole cranberry sauce while water is still hot to help dissolve the sauce. Cut plums in half; pit. Add plums and juice to gelatin mixture, stirring well to blend. Add pecans. Pour into a square pan (or crown mold, if preferred) that has been rinsed with cold water. Chill until set. To serve, cut into squares and serve on lettuce leaf with small dollop of salad dressing to garnish. Makes 8 to 12 servings.

VEGETABLES

Asparagus Casserole

½ pound medium sharp cheddar cheese, shredded
2 cups soda cracker crumbs
½ cup butter, melted
2 14½-ounce cans cut asparagus or comparable
* amount of fresh*
1 10¾-ounce can cream of mushroom soup
1 cup slivered almonds

Preheat oven to 350°. Mix cheese, cracker crumbs and melted butter. Press firmly in the bottom of a buttered 8x10-inch glass casserole dish. Add asparagus liquid to the soup. Arrange asparagus over the cracker crust and pour soup mixture evenly over all; sprinkle with nuts. Bake for 30 minutes. After removing from oven, set aside for a few minutes before serving. Makes 10 generous servings.

Boozed Baked Beans

6 slices bacon
1 large onion, chopped
1 medium green pepper, chopped
2 16-ounce cans pork and beans
¼ cup firmly packed brown sugar
1 teaspoon Worcestershire sauce
1 teaspoon dry mustard
1 cup catsup
1 tablespoon molasses
¼ cup Jack Daniel's Whiskey

Preheat oven to 350°. Cook bacon in skillet until done but not yet crisp. Remove bacon from pan, dice and set aside. Drain all but 2 tablespoons drippings. Add onion and pepper; sauté until soft. Combine all ingredients, except bacon, in a 1-quart casserole. Top with bacon. Bake for 40 to 45 minutes. Makes 8 servings.

Orange Beets

18 to 20 small beets
2 tablespoons cornstarch
1 cup firmly packed light brown sugar
1 6-ounce can frozen orange juice concentrate
¾ cup cider vinegar
2 tablespoons butter

Cut the tops from the beets and wash. Cover with water and bring to a boil. Lower heat, cover and simmer until beets are tender (30 minutes or longer depending on the age of the beets). Drain, reserving 1 cup of cooking liquid. Cool beets; peel and set aside. In a saucepan, combine cornstarch, brown sugar, juice, vinegar and reserved liquid. Heat until thickened and clear, stirring often. Add butter and whole beets. Heat thoroughly before serving. Makes 6 servings.

Beet and Carrot Purée

1 pound beets
1 pound carrots
3 tablespoons butter
Salt
Pepper

In a saucepan, cook unpeeled beets in boiling water until tender. Cool, peel and quarter. Put in a food processor fitted with the steel blade. Scrape the carrots; cook in boiling water until tender. Add to beets in processor. Process until mixture is a smooth purée. Add butter, salt and pepper to taste. Makes 4 servings.

Harvard Beets

2 tablespoons butter
1 tablespoon cornstarch
3 tablespoons sugar
¼ teaspoon salt
⅓ cup vinegar
2 cups small whole beets, cooked or canned

Melt butter in saucepan; add cornstarch, sugar and salt. Blend in vinegar; heat, stirring constantly, until thick. Add beets; heat thoroughly. Makes 4 to 6 servings.

Spiced Garden Beets

2 bunches fresh beets (about 3½ pounds)
1½ teaspoons salt
⅔ cup sugar
1 teaspoon ground cinnamon
½ teaspoon ground cloves
⅔ cup apple cider vinegar
2 large onions, sliced

Cut off the greens from beets and discard; leave about 1 inch of stem. Wash beets and place in large saucepan. Add cold water to cover. Bring to a boil and add salt. Continue to boil in partially covered pan until beets are tender, about 35 minutes. Drain and cool. When cool enough to hold, cut off stems and slip off skins. Cut beets into chunks or slices. In large stainless steel pan (not aluminum), combine sugar, spices, vinegar and ½ cup water. Bring to a boil; add beets, lower heat and simmer for 5 minutes. Remove from heat and add onion slices. Place in serving dish; cover and chill. Makes 10 servings.

BROCCOLI AND RICE CASSEROLE

Helen Daniel is a retired cook from Miss Bobo's Boarding House. Helen was a wonderful cook and seldom got ruffled or flustered. However, one day when the cooks were preparing for a big dinner, Helen accidentally poured lemonade instead of buttermilk in the cornbread. The hoots, howls and laughter broke all the tension that had built up in the hot kitchen and the rest of the day went without a hitch. Still, until the day she retired, no one let her forget that she was the one who goofed on cornbread when the going got tough. Here is Helen's favorite Broccoli and Rice Casserole.

1 large onion, chopped
½ cup butter
1 10-ounce package frozen chopped broccoli
1 cup quick-cooking rice, uncooked
1 10¾-ounce can cream of chicken soup
½ cup milk
1 cup shredded cheese

Preheat oven to 350°. Sauté onion in butter; add broccoli, rice, soup, milk and half the cheese. Pour into a greased 2-quart casserole. Bake for 20 to 25 minutes. Top with remaining cheese and bake 10 minutes longer. Makes 4 to 6 servings.

BRUSSELS SPROUTS IN CELERY SAUCE

1 pound Brussels sprouts, washed and trimmed
1½ cups chopped celery
3 tablespoons butter
3 tablespoons all-purpose flour
1 cup milk
Celery salt and pepper to taste

Cook sprouts in boiling salted water until tender. Drain. Cook celery in salted water until tender; drain and reserve ½ cup celery water. Melt butter in heavy saucepan. Add flour; mix celery water with milk. Stir into flour mixture; heat until sauce is thickened. Season with celery salt and pepper. Add celery; pour over hot Brussels sprouts. Makes 6 servings.

BRAISED CABBAGE

1 head cabbage
2 carrots, chopped
1 onion, chopped
2 tablespoons butter
¾ cup chicken broth
½ cup water
Pepper
Salt

Remove outer leaves and core from cabbage; shred. In a heavy saucepan, sauté onion and carrots in butter just until tender. Add cabbage and toss. Add broth and water. Season with salt and pepper to taste. Simmer, covered, for 12 to 15 minutes or until cabbage is tender. Add extra broth as needed during cooking process. Makes 6 servings.

MISS MARY'S CABBAGE CASSEROLE

½ head of cabbage, chopped
1 small onion, chopped
½ green pepper, chopped
3 tablespoons butter or margarine
3 tablespoons all-purpose flour
1 cup milk
½ cup shredded cheddar cheese
  Cornbread crumbs

Cook the first 3 ingredients in lightly salted water until tender. Drain. Melt butter in saucepan. Stir in flour and cook for 1 minute, stirring constantly. Slowly add milk; stir until thickened. Add cheese; blend until melted. Preheat oven to 325°. Layer the drained cabbage mixture and cheese sauce in a greased casserole. Make several layers ending with sauce. Bake until bubbly. Top with crumbs (we use cornbread crumbs that are sprinkled with poultry seasoning, or you could use cornbread stuffing mix). Return to oven until lightly browned. Makes 4 servings.

CABBAGE CUSTARD

   1 2-pound head cabbage, cored
1½ cups soft bread crumbs
   2 cups grated sharp cheddar cheese
   3 eggs
   1 teaspoon salt
   2 tablespoons Dijon-style mustard
   2 cups milk

Shred cabbage (should be 4 cups) and place in a large saucepan. Cover with water and bring to a boil. Cook just until tender. Drain. In a 2-quart buttered casserole, layer half the cabbage. Combine bread crumbs and cheese. Sprinkle half over the cabbage. Repeat layers. Beat together eggs, salt and mustard. Add milk. Pour mixture over cabbage. Set aside for 20 minutes. Preheat oven to 350°. Bake for 30 minutes. Makes 6 to 8 servings.

RED CABBAGE AND APPLES

   1 head red cabbage
   1 onion, chopped
¼ cup bacon drippings
½ cup red wine
½ cup water
¼ cup red wine vinegar
   3 tablespoons brown sugar
   2 tart apples, peeled, cored and sliced

Remove outer leaves and core from cabbage; shred. In a heavy saucepan, sauté onion in bacon drippings until tender. Add shredded cabbage. Toss. Combine wine, water, vinegar and brown sugar and pour over cabbage. Add sliced apples. Cook over low heat, covered, for 1½ to 2 hours, depending on freshness of cabbage. Check occasionally to be sure that all liquid has not boiled away; add more red wine or water if necessary. Toss before serving. The apples will have dissolved into the cabbage. Makes 6 servings.

CARROT-SWEET POTATO RING

   1 large onion, chopped
   2 tablespoons butter
   1 pound carrots, cooked and mashed
   1 pound sweet potatoes, cooked and mashed
   1 egg, beaten
   1 tablespoon grated orange rind
¼ cup honey
⅓ cup Jack Daniel's Whiskey

Preheat oven to 350°. Sauté onion in butter. In a bowl, mix mashed carrots and sweet potatoes; stir in onion and remaining ingredients. Spoon into well-greased ring mold. Bake for 20 to 25 minutes or until firm. Unmold. Fill center with cooked green vegetables. Makes 6 servings.

GARDEN CARROT CASSEROLE

   2 pounds carrots, scraped and cut into rounds
   3 tablespoons butter
   1 large onion, chopped
   4 tablespoons all-purpose flour
   2 cups milk
1½ cups shredded sharp cheddar cheese
   1 teaspoon dry mustard
½ teaspoon celery salt
   Cracker crumbs
   Butter

Cook carrots in lightly salted water until tender. Drain. Sauté onion in butter until tender. Stir in flour; slowly add milk. Cook over medium heat until thickened. Add cheddar cheese, mustard and celery salt. Stir until cheese is melted. Preheat oven to 325°. Layer carrots with cheese sauce in greased casserole. Top with cracker crumbs. Dot with butter. Bake until browned and bubbly. Makes 6 to 8 servings.

Music Fills the Air

I f the words of a song could describe Tennessee, then the following nine words from the popular musical say it all: "The hills are alive with the sound of music." From the mountain music of East Tennessee to the blues and jazzier tunes of the Mississippi Delta land, right down to the very heart of the music industry in Nashville, music is a Tennessee tradition. People who settled in these parts love music and have made their mark on the world with the music they have created.

From the hills of Ireland and Scotland, settlers came with their haunting tunes and highland flings. From southern Europe came folk singers with stories repeated in song. From Africa came slaves with spiritual chants and soul-wrenching wails. From the Caribbean and coastal regions came light-hearted calypso beats. All of these cultures can be heard in the music that evolved from early Tennessee. It is the very root of our American southland music.

Instruments, which were not in great supply, were made at home in the hope of recreating the sounds settlers remembered from their motherland. Added to the stringed instruments were saws, Jew's-harps, jugs and spoons for rhythm. When nothing else was available, music makers slapped their pants legs and used washboards and washtubs. Music was heard in every hollow.

Through hard times and good times, man's condition in the world was expressed in every word. Deep religious beliefs were expressed in spirituals, Bible stories were recounted in lyrics for all to learn and the gospel expressed joy in song. Heroes and hangings, fun times and sad times, marching-off-to-war times and praises-for-peace times are what the people sang about.

Whether mountain or country, blues or bluegrass, gospel or spiritual, music is the root and soul of Tennessee.

MARINATED CARROTS

2 pounds carrots
1 10¾-ounce can tomato soup
½ cup vegetable oil
½ cup sugar
1 teaspoon Worcestershire sauce
¾ cup vinegar
1 teaspoon prepared mustard
    Salt and pepper to taste
1 green pepper, chopped
1 onion, chopped

Wash and scrape carrots and cut into rounds. Cook in water just until tender. Drain. Mix soup, oil, sugar, Worcestershire sauce, vinegar, mustard and seasonings. Add carrots, green pepper, and onion. Chill overnight before serving.

(This will keep a week or more.) Makes 8 to 10 servings.

CREOLE CAULIFLOWER AU GRATIN

4 tablespoons butter
½ cup chopped onion
½ cup chopped green pepper
3 tablespoons all-purpose flour
2 cups canned tomatoes, lightly drained and chopped
    Salt and pepper to taste
3 cups cooked cauliflower
½ cup grated cheese

Preheat oven to 350°. Melt butter in saucepan; sauté onion and green pepper until tender. Stir in flour. Add tomatoes; cook until thickened. Season with salt and pepper. Add cauliflower and heat thoroughly. Spoon into casserole dish; top with cheese. Bake until cheese is melted. Makes 6 servings.

WASH DAY CASSEROLE

¼ cup butter
5 eggs
¼ cup all-purpose flour
½ teaspoon baking powder
    Dash of salt
1 16-ounce can corn, cream-style or whole kernel
1 cup cottage cheese
½ pound grated cheese, jack, cheddar or hoop
½ cup chopped green pepper

Preheat oven to 400°. In a 9-inch cast iron skillet, slowly melt butter, turning pan to coat sides and bottom. Mix eggs with fork until light and creamy. Add remaining ingredients and mix just until blended. Pour into prepared skillet or casserole, if preferred. Bake for 10 minutes. Reduce heat to 350° and bake 35 minutes longer (or until set). Can be served hot or cold. Makes 6 servings.

COUNTRY FRIED CORN

Fresh vegetables are the specialty of Miss Mary Bobo's Boarding house in Lynchburg. During the season, vegetables are picked fresh in the morning from the gardens out back and cooked to serve that day. The flavor of fresh vegetables is hard to describe and impossible to beat.

Cooks in this area have created some wonderful recipes to take advantage of peak season bounty. Here is one such recipe to add variety and enjoyment to your meal. It is a favorite of guests at Miss Mary's.

6 ears fresh corn
3 slices country bacon, pork side meat or, best of all, country ham fat
⅔ cup water
2 tablespoons sugar
¼ cup milk
2 teaspoons cornstarch
1 tablespoon butter
Salt to taste

In large bowl, use a sharp knife to cut tips of kernels from ears of corn. Scrape cobs with knife to get out all the juice. Set aside. Cook bacon in heavy skillet until crisp (if using side meat or ham fat, cook until fat is rendered); remove from skillet and reserve. Stir corn into hot bacon drippings; add water and sugar. Cook, stirring constantly, until mixture begins to thicken. Gradually stir milk into cornstarch until smooth. Add cornstarch mixture to corn; cook over low heat until thickened. Stir in butter and salt. Serve topped with reserved crumbled bacon. Makes 6 servings.

SOUTHERN GREENS WITH POT LIQUOR

1 ham hock or 4 strips bacon or 2 ounces diced salt pork
2 cups water

1 pound turnip greens, mustard greens, collard greens or kale
½ teaspoon red pepper flakes
Salt and pepper

Simmer ham hock in water until tender. Add water as needed to maintain two cups. (If using bacon or salt pork, fry in heavy saucepan until crisp. Remove bacon or pieces of salt pork from drippings. Add water to rendered fat.) Carefully wash greens, removing tough stems and blemished areas. Add greens to liquid; add red pepper flakes. Simmer, covered, for 25 to 35 minutes or until tender. Season with salt and pepper to taste. If ham hock was used, remove skin, bones and fat. Return pieces of lean ham to greens. This is delicious served with cornbread. Makes 4 to 6 servings.

FRIED HOMINY GRITS

1 cup hominy grits
4 cups cold water
1 teaspoon salt
¼ teaspoon sugar
1 egg
1 tablespoon milk
All-purpose flour

Add the grits to the water and bring to a boil. Add salt and sugar. Lower heat and cook for 1 hour, stirring often. Remove from heat and drain off any liquid. Pour into buttered loaf pan. Cover and chill overnight. Unmold and cut into ½-inch thick slices. Beat together egg and milk. Dredge each slice of grits with flour, then dip in the egg batter. Fry on greased griddle until slices are golden brown. Serve with maple syrup or jelly for breakfast. Makes 4 to 6 servings.

TENNESSEE WILD MUSHROOMS GRATIN

This recipe is the creation of Executive Chef Robert Siegel, of Maude's Courtyard Restaurant in Nashville, Tennessee.

It can be prepared as an appetizer or used as a side dish with any meat, game or poultry.

2 teaspoons chopped garlic
4 tablespoons chopped shallots
1 pound sliced exotic mushrooms*
2 tablespoons butter
¼ cup white wine
¼ cup Jack Daniel's Whiskey
2 cups heavy cream
1 teaspoon salt
½ teaspoon black pepper
¼ cup grated Parmesan cheese
¼ cup grated Swiss cheese
¼ cup bread crumbs

Sauté the garlic, shallots and mushrooms in butter for 5 minutes until they start to soften. Add the wine, Jack Daniel's Whiskey and heavy cream. Simmer for 5 minutes longer. Remove mushrooms with a slotted spoon and place onto 4 serving dishes; leave the pan liquid over the burner to reduce. Reduce the liquid until it forms a thick sauce; season with salt and pepper and pour over the mushrooms. Combine cheeses and crumbs. Top each mushroom dish with the cheese and crumb mixture and place under the broiler until browned. Makes 4 servings.

Note: Many grocery stores are now stocking new varieties of mushrooms, including shitake, enoki, porchini or morels. All of these are excellent, as well as the commonly cultivated white mushrooms.

MUSHROOMS IN CREAM SAUCE

2 tablespoons butter
1 pound mushrooms, sliced
2 tablespoons chopped chives
3 tablespoons Jack Daniel's Whiskey
½ cup light cream
2 tablespoons catsup
½ teaspoon salt
⅛ teaspoon pepper
Toast points

Melt butter in large skillet; sauté mushrooms and chives over low heat. When mushrooms are browned and tender, add Jack Daniel's Whiskey. Carefully ignite and shake pan until flames go out. Stir in cream, catsup, salt and pepper. Cook just until mixture begins to boil, stirring constantly. Serve on toast points. Makes 4 servings.

FRESH OKRA AND TOMATO BAKE

⅓ cup butter
½ cup chopped green pepper

½ cup chopped onion
2 tablespoons all-purpose flour
1 teaspoon salt
½ teaspoon pepper
1 teaspoon sugar
2 cups chopped tomatoes
1¼ cups sliced okra
½ teaspoon dried basil leaves
4 slices American cheese, cut into triangles

Preheat oven to 325°. Melt butter in large skillet. Sauté green pepper and onion until soft. Stir in flour, salt, pepper and sugar. Add tomatoes, okra and basil. Pour mixture into a lightly greased 1½-quart baking dish; top with cheese slices. Bake for 25 to 30 minutes or until bubbly. Makes 6 servings.

ONION AND APPLE BAKE

2 large onions, peeled and sliced
2 medium apples, peeled, cored and sliced
4 slices bacon, cooked crisp and crumbled
1 tablespoon bacon drippings
⅓ cup soft bread crumbs
½ cup chicken stock

Preheat oven to 350°. Grease a baking dish. Layer onion slices, apple slices and bacon in dish. Heat bacon drippings; stir in bread crumbs until drippings are absorbed. Set aside. Pour chicken stock over casserole. Bake, covered, for 30 minutes. Remove from oven and top with bread crumbs. Continue to bake, uncovered, 15 minutes longer. This is a delicious side dish with roast pork. Makes 2 to 3 servings.

BAKED ONIONS WITH HAM STUFFING

6 small onions, peeled
3 tablespoons butter
2 tomatoes, peeled, seeded and finely chopped

1½ cups finely chopped cooked ham
2 tablespoons tomato purée
¼ teaspoon powdered thyme
½ teaspoon salt
¼ teaspoon pepper
½ cup grated Monterey Jack cheese
2 tablespoons butter
1 cup chicken broth

Preheat oven to 400°. Parboil peeled onions for 10 minutes in boiling water. Drain. Cut a slice from the top of each and remove all but ¾-inch of outer shell. Chop the removed pulp and sauté in butter until tender. Add tomatoes and sauté a few minutes; add ham, tomato purée, thyme, salt and pepper. Fill the onion shells with mixture and top with grated cheese. Dot with butter. Place the onions in a shallow, greased pan and pour broth in the bottom. Bake for 30 minutes, basting occasionally with broth. Makes 6 servings.

ONION CASSEROLE

8 onions
1 cup bread crumbs
½ teaspoon salt
½ teaspoon paprika
1 tablespoon butter
1 cup chopped pecans
1 tablespoon butter
1 tablespoon all-purpose flour
1 cup milk
½ teaspoon salt

Preheat oven to 350°. Peel onions and boil whole in salted water for 15 minutes or until partially cooked. Cool; remove centers, chop and combine with next 5 ingredients. Stuff onion shells with mixture. Melt remaining butter; stir in flour. Cook for 30 seconds, stirring constantly. Add milk and salt. Stir over heat until thickened. Place onions in buttered baking dish. Pour sauce over onions. Bake 30 minutes. Makes 8 servings.

Mules, Mules, Mules

Moore County is where Tennessee Blue Grass meets the Cumberland Mountains. It is the finest and, some say, the most productive grassland in all the state. People grow crops, raise cattle, breed hound dogs and mules in this fertile and productive area. Early on, mule trading was big business in this part of the world. No wonder that Lem Motlow went to buying and selling mules when prohibition went into effect. With his distillery closed, Mr. Lem looked for another lucrative business. At that time farmers still plowed their ground with a mule-pulled bull-tongue plow. Although the land is fertile, many crops are grown on the side of a ridge or the slope of a mountain. A farmer needed a good mule or mule team.

In April of every year, farmers went to Tullahoma or Columbia where mule trading was a big event. Traders lined up the mules placing the most expensive animals next to the courthouse and the cheaper ones further away. At the end of the line, men would trade a hound dog for a mule, and there was controversy as to who got the best deal. Once Mr. Lem Motlow assembled more than 3,000 mules for trading and auction in Lynchburg. It was said to be the biggest event ever held there.

On October 26, 1985, in memory of this event and to celebrate the 200th anniversary of the first mule in America (The first mule to arrive on American soil was a gift from King Charles III of Spain in 1785 to George Washington.), the Jack Daniel Distillery decided to have a "Mule Appreciation Day Celebration" in Lynchburg. It invited mule breeders to bring their mules for showing, judging, trading and selling. Mule teams with silver harnesses, fancy rigs of all sizes, and matching pairs and matching teams came from all over. One man shipped his twenty-mule team and wagon from California for the event. Needless to say, this was the biggest event ever to be held in Lynchburg. And you didn't have to be a jackass to have a grand time.

Lynchburg, Tennessee, *circa* 1923

SOUSED ONIONS

This is a sweet and tangy relish. Delicious with paté, cold sliced meats or with hors d'oeuvres.

¼ cup golden raisins
¼ cup Jack Daniel's Whiskey
1 pound small white onions or pearl onions
3 tablespoons vegetable oil
4 teaspoons brown sugar
3 large tomatoes, peeled, seeded and chopped
¼ teaspoon salt
¼ teaspoon dried thyme or large sprig fresh thyme
½ teaspoon freshly ground pepper

Preheat oven to 350°. Soak raisins in ¼ cup Jack Daniel's Whiskey. Peel and clean onions. In large skillet, over medium heat, sauté onions in oil. Shake the pan until onions are golden brown, about 5 minutes. Sprinkle brown sugar over onions; reduce heat to low. Cook until onions are caramelized, about 5 minutes. Add tomatoes and salt; cook 5 minutes longer. Add raisins, Jack Daniel's Whiskey, thyme and pepper. Transfer the mixture to a small casserole. Cover; bake for 1½ hours. Remove from oven. Adjust seasoning, if needed. Cool; refrigerate overnight. Bring to room temperature before serving. Makes approximately 4 cups.

PINEAPPLE-CHEDDAR CASSEROLE

1 20-ounce can pineapple chunks, preferably juice packed
2 tablespoons all-purpose flour
2 tablespoons sugar
1¼ cups shredded cheddar cheese
1½ cups (about 25) crushed Ritz crackers
3 tablespoons butter, melted

Preheat oven to 350°. Drain the pineapple, reserving 3 tablespoons juice. Arrange the pineapple on the bottom of a greased 1½-quart cas-serole. Combine the flour and sugar; sprinkle over the pineapple. Drizzle the reserved pineapple liquid over top; sprinkle with cheddar cheese. Combine the crackers and melted butter; sprinkle over cheese. Bake, covered, for 15 minutes. Uncover and bake 10 minutes longer. Makes 6 to 8 servings.

SOUTHERN BELLE FANCY POTATOES

1½ cups large curd cottage cheese
1 cup sour cream
1 cup chopped green onions
1 clove garlic, minced
1 teaspoon salt
5 cups peeled, diced and cooked potatoes
½ cup grated cheddar cheese
Paprika

Preheat oven to 350°. Combine cottage cheese, sour cream, onion, garlic and salt. Fold in potatoes. Spoon into a greased 2-quart casserole. Top with cheese and sprinkle with paprika. Bake 30 to 40 minutes. Makes 6 to 8 servings.

GOLDEN POTATO CAKE

2 pounds potatoes
6 tablespoons butter, divided
2 cups shredded cheese, Gruyère or Swiss
Salt and pepper to taste
1½ cups chicken stock

Peel and thinly slice potatoes. Soak in ice water for 30 minutes. Drain. Preheat oven to 425°. Grease a shallow round ovenproof baking dish with 3 tablespoons butter. Arrange ⅓ of the potato slices, overlapping, in dish; cover with half the cheese. Repeat layers. Cover with remaining third of the potato slices. Season with salt and pepper (be careful not to oversalt if stock is already salty).

Pour stock over dish. Cover and bake for 1 hour. Uncover and bake 30 minutes longer. Cut into wedges to serve. Makes 6 servings.

Motlow Family & Distillery Workers (*circa* 1910). Lem Motlow (he's seated in the front and wearing suspenders) with three of his sons: Robert, D.E. (Hap) and Reagor. His two brothers, Jess and Tom, are also in the center front.

The teamsters (at right) picked up the barrels of whiskey to be shipped out of Tullahoma by railroad. The roads at that time were all dirt and for the most part very bad. They drove six-mule-team wagons. The drivers would ride on the lead left mule with one guide rope and were so proficient they could drive a team through a gate with barely a foot clearance at full speed and not hesitate a moment.

MASHED POTATO CASSEROLE

6 medium potatoes, peeled
¼ cup finely chopped onion
½ cup sour cream
¼ cup grated Parmesan cheese
Salt
Pepper
¼ cup bread crumbs
Butter

Preheat oven to 400°. Cook potatoes in boiling water until tender. Drain and mash. Add onion, sour cream, and cheese. Season with salt and pepper to taste. Pour into greased 1½-quart casserole. Sprinkle with bread crumbs and dot with butter. Bake until lightly browned. Makes 6 servings.

NUTTY STEWED PRUNES

Butter
1 pound prunes, pitted
1 cup pecan halves
1 cup firmly packed light brown sugar
1 cup water
1 lemon, seeded and thinly sliced
⅓ cup Jack Daniel's Whiskey

Preheat oven to 350°. Generously grease a pie pan with butter. Stuff a pecan half in each prune and arrange prunes in pie pan. Chop remaining pecans and sprinkle over the prunes. Combine brown sugar, water and lemon slices in a saucepan. Bring to a boil; cook for several minutes. Strain liquid over prunes. Bake prunes for 20 minutes; cover with drained lemon slices, and bake for 10 minutes longer. Heat Jack Daniel's Whiskey in a small pan, carefully ignite and let the flame burn out. Pour over the prunes. Discard lemon slices and serve prunes warm. This is delicious as a side dish with pork. Makes 8 servings.

REBEL RAISINS

2½ cups raisins
3 tablespoons butter
2 tablespoons all-purpose flour
3 tablespoons brown sugar
2 tablespoons lemon juice

In a heavy saucepan, barely cover raisins with water and bring to a boil. Lower heat and simmer 20 minutes or until water begins to evaporate. Add butter. Stir together flour and sugar and sprinkle over raisins stirring constantly. Cook until thickened. Add lemon juice. Serve with baked ham. Makes 2½ cups.

SAVANNAH RED RICE

6 slices bacon
2 green peppers, chopped
2 onions, chopped

2 cups cooked rice
1 16-ounce can stewed tomatoes
1 cup tomato sauce
½ teaspoon red pepper flakes
  Salt and pepper to taste
  Ham, cooked shrimp or sausage, optional
¼ cup Parmesan cheese, grated

Preheat oven to 350°. In a large skillet, fry bacon until crisp. Remove; chop when cool. Reserve drippings. Sauté green pepper and onion in drippings until tender. Add rice, tomatoes, tomato sauce, red pepper flakes and bacon. Season with salt and pepper. If using meat or fish, add now. Spoon into a greased 2-quart baking dish. Sprinkle Parmesan cheese over top. Bake 25 to 30 minutes or until rice is dry. Makes 4 servings.

SPINACH-ARTICHOKE-MUSHROOM CASSEROLE

1 pound fresh mushrooms, sliced
8 tablespoons butter, divided
2 tablespoons all-purpose flour
1 cup milk, heated
  Salt and pepper to taste
2 10-ounce boxes frozen spinach, chopped, thawed and drained
1 1-pound can artichoke hearts, drained and chopped
½ cup sour cream
½ cup mayonnaise
2 tablespoons lemon juice
  Nutmeg

In a large skillet, sauté mushrooms in 6 tablespoons butter; remove mushrooms and set aside. Add remaining 2 tablespoons butter to drippings in skillet; when melted, stir in flour and cook until bubbly. Add milk and stir until mixture is smooth. Add salt, pepper, spinach and mushrooms. Cook over medium heat 10 minutes. Preheat oven to 350°. Cover bottom of an oblong baking dish with artichoke hearts. Pour spinach mixture over artichoke hearts. Mix sour cream, mayonnaise and

lemon juice; spread over top of spinach mixture. Sprinkle with nutmeg. Bake, covered, for 30 minutes. Makes 8 servings.

SPINACH RING MOLD

2 10-ounce packages frozen chopped spinach
3 eggs, separated
2 cups milk
1½ cups cracker crumbs
1 small onion, chopped
1 clove garlic, minced
½ teaspoon salt
½ teaspoon pepper
¾ cup butter, melted
  Harvard Beets (see recipe on page 58)

Preheat oven to 350°. Thaw frozen spinach; drain and press dry. Blend egg yolks and milk; add spinach, crumbs, onion, garlic, salt, pepper and butter. Beat egg whites until stiff but not dry. Fold whites into spinach mixture. Pour into a greased 1½-quart ring mold. Place mold into a larger shallow pan containing hot water. Bake for 45 minutes or until set. Cool for 15 minutes before unmolding onto serving dish. Fill center of ring with Harvard Beets. Makes 6 to 8 servings.

SASSY SWEET POTATO PONE

1 cup sugar
1 cup (2 sticks) butter, melted
2 cups grated uncooked sweet potatoes
½ cup half-and-half
1 teaspoon ground ginger
  Grated rind of 1 orange

Preheat oven to 350°. Stir together sugar and butter. Add grated sweet potatoes, half-and-half, ginger and orange rind. Pour into a greased 1-quart casserole. Bake until firm and golden brown. Makes 4 servings.

Fall Festival Squash

6 acorn squash
¼ cup water
2 tablespoons butter
1 tablespoon brown sugar
¼ teaspoon cinnamon
    Salt to taste
2 tablespoons Jack Daniel's Whiskey

Preheat oven to 325°. Halve squash lengthwise; scrape seed and fibers from cavities. Place squash, cut-side down in baking dish with water. Bake for 1 hour. Scoop out pulp and reserve six of the best shells. Mash cooked pulp with remaining ingredients, beating well. Spoon mixture into reserved shells. Bake until hot. Makes 6 servings.

Tipsy Sweet Potatoes

2½ cups cooked, mashed sweet potatoes
4 tablespoons butter, softened
½ cup firmly packed light brown sugar
    Pinch of salt
⅓ cup Jack Daniel's Whiskey
    Pecan halves or marshmallow for topping

Preheat oven to 325°. Combine all ingredients except topping. Spoon into a greased 1-quart casserole. Top with pecan halves or marshmallows. Bake for 20 to 25 minutes until bubbly. Makes 6 to 8 servings, but be careful, everyone will want seconds!

Cheese-Fried Green Tomatoes

½ cup yellow cornmeal
½ cup finely grated Swiss cheese
½ teaspoon salt
¼ teaspoon pepper
½ cup all-purpose flour
2 eggs
3 medium green tomatoes (about 1¼ pounds), cored and cut into ¼-inch slices
4 to 6 tablespoons vegetable oil, divided
    Salt

Combine cornmeal, cheese, salt and pepper in shallow dish. Place flour on waxed paper. Beat eggs lightly in a separate dish. Dredge tomato slices in flour, shaking off excess. Dip in beaten egg, then in cornmeal mixture; press cornmeal lightly onto both sides. Place on wire rack. (At this point the tomato slices can be set aside for several hours.) Heat 3 tablespoons of oil in large skillet over moderately high heat until very hot. Place a layer of tomato slices in skillet without overcrowding. Fry on both sides until crisp and golden, about 2 minutes per side. Drain on paper towels; sprinkle with salt. Keep warm. Fry remaining slices, adding more oil as needed. Serve warm. Makes 4 servings.

Stewed Tomato Casserole

1 28-ounce can tomatoes, undrained and coarsely chopped
2 tablespoons butter or margarine
⅓ cup sugar
2 slices white bread, toasted and crumbled

Preheat oven to 350°. Place the tomatoes, butter and sugar in a saucepan; heat until the butter is melted. Add the bread crumbs; simmer until most of the liquid is absorbed, about 15 minutes. Spoon the mixture into a greased 1½-quart round casserole. Bake about 20 to 30 minutes or until thick and bubbly. Makes 6 servings.

Unusual Tomato-Apple Casserole

4 cups canned tomatoes, drained
3 cups cubed dry toast
¼ cup chopped fresh parsley
1 tablespoon minced garlic
6 tablespoons butter, divided
1 teaspoon ground cinnamon
½ teaspoon sugar
¼ teaspoon pepper
3 apples, peeled, cored and sliced
2 cups grated Mozzarella cheese

Preheat oven to 350°. Squeeze seeds out of tomatoes and place in colander to drain. Sauté toast cubes, parsley and garlic in 4 tablespoons butter until all the butter has been absorbed. Combine crouton mixture, tomatoes, cinnamon, sugar and pepper. In a 2½-quart baking dish, layer tomato mixture, apple slices and cheese. Repeat layers ending with apples. Dot top with remaining butter. Bake 30 to 35 minutes. Garnish with additional Mozzarella cheese, if desired. Makes 8 servings.

Tomato Pudding

¼ cup butter
2 cups cubed white bread
1 10-ounce can whole tomatoes, undrained
⅓ cup firmly packed light brown sugar
¼ teaspoon salt
½ teaspoon dried basil

Preheat oven to 325°. Melt butter. Pour over bread cubes and toss. Drain the tomatoes and reserve the liquid. Chop the tomatoes. In a saucepan, heat the tomatoes, tomato juice, sugar, salt and basil. Bring to a boil and simmer for 5 minutes. Pour tomato mixture over bread cubes and toss. Place mixture in a greased 1½-quart casserole and bake for 40 to 45 minutes. This is a delicious side dish with pork or chicken. Makes 6 servings.

Summertime Tomato-Cheese Casserole

3 cups thinly sliced onions
1 cup soft bread crumbs
1 teaspoon salt
½ teaspoon pepper
4 large ripe tomatoes, peeled and sliced
1½ cups grated sharp cheddar cheese
   Salt and pepper to taste
3 tablespoons butter

Preheat oven to 375°. Blanch onion in boiling water and cover for 5 minutes. Drain. Combine bread crumbs, salt and pepper. Butter a 2-quart baking dish. Layer half the tomato slices in the bottom, top with half the cooked sliced onion, half the bread crumbs and half the cheese. Sprinkle with salt and pepper and repeat layers. Dot with butter. Bake for 40 to 45 minutes. Makes 4 to 6 servings.

White Turnip Casserole

3 pounds fresh white turnips
   Bacon drippings
¼ cup butter, melted
2 teaspoons sugar
1 teaspoon salt
¼ teaspoon pepper
3 eggs
1 teaspoon vinegar
1 cup bread crumbs
   Paprika

Peel and dice turnips. Cook in boiling salted water seasoned with bacon drippings until turnips are tender. Drain. Preheat oven to 375°. Combine butter, sugar, salt, pepper, eggs and vinegar; stir into diced turnips. Blend in bread crumbs. Spoon into greased casserole. Sprinkle with paprika. Bake for 40 to 45 minutes. Makes 8 servings.

Mr. Jack Daniel's Original Silver Cornet Band

Hometown Homecoming

FEATURING Mr. JACK DANIEL'S ORIGINAL SILVER CORNET BAND

IN CONCERT

The period from 1876 until World War I was the Era of Small Town Bands in America. Now, no one at the time knew this; they just knew that their hometown band was as close as they were going to get to big city culture. At the time, America was a young nation, a string of rural towns. Townspeople—the banker, the shopkeeper, the barber, the farmer—learned to play an instrument and performed with the town band for hometown celebrations, saloon openings, mule auctions, or afternoons in the park bandstand. There were 10,000 of these bands in 1892, and one was in Lynchburg, Tennessee. Mr. Jack Daniel, hometown benefactor, had purchased silver cornets and a variety of other instruments for about $300, a substantial outlay at the time.

In 1973 the band was recreated to present a program about this era for PBS television. The program depicted a quiet and unruffled time in our history when there were no telephones, radios, television, computer games or electric instruments. The band played Sousa marches, Cohan show tunes, Joplin rags and other popular tunes of the day. Medleys of Gilbert and Sullivan operettas and even Rossini arias were performed with beauty and skill. Music of the period in the sound of the period, all costumed in suits of the nineties and presented in a gazebo—the show was an instant hit.

Today the band has performed three PBS television specials, completed twenty national tours and recorded eight albums. It has made appearances at Avery Fisher Hall in Lincoln Center, on the NBC "Today Show," on The Nashville Network and at the White House.

Members of Mr. Jack Daniel's Original Silver Cornet Band are ambassadors for Tennessee and for Lynchburg, spreading the spirit of our American heritage in story and music. Lynchburg is proud to claim them as their own.

JACK DANIEL'S SWEET MOORE COUNTY WILD RICE

¼ cup Jack Daniel's Whiskey
1 6¼-ounce package long grain and wild rice mix
1 tablespoon butter
1 can sliced peaches, drained and chopped
⅓ cup coarsely chopped toasted pecans

Add enough water to Jack Daniel's Whiskey to make 2⅓ cups liquid. Combine with rice seasoning packets and butter. Bring to a boil. Add rice, cover and simmer until liquid is absorbed, about 25 minutes. Stir in peaches and pecans; heat through. Makes 4 servings.

ZUCCHINI AU GRATIN

8 young, tender zucchini
4 green onions, finely chopped
3 tablespoons butter
¼ cup chopped fresh parsley
¼ cup chopped fresh dill (or 1 teaspoon dried dill)
⅔ cup sour cream
*   Salt and pepper*
6 tablespoons bread crumbs
2 tablespoons grated Parmesan cheese

Preheat oven to 350°. Wash zucchini, but do not peel. Grate and place in colander to drain for 30 minutes. Sauté onion in half the butter until tender. Add drained zucchini, parsley and dill. Cook until zucchini begins to wilt. Remove from heat and stir in sour cream. Add salt and pepper to taste. Pour into baking dish. Top with bread crumbs mixed with cheese. Dot with remaining butter. Bake for 25 to 30 minutes or until brown and bubbly. Makes 6 servings.

SOMETHING DIFFERENT TO DO WITH ZUCCHINI

1¼ cups all-purpose flour
½ teaspoon salt
½ teaspoon crushed anise seed
½ cup butter
½ cup grated cheddar cheese
½ cup finely chopped onion
2 cloves garlic, minced
2 tablespoons bacon drippings
2 cups thinly sliced zucchini
6 eggs, beaten
1 cup sour cream
1 teaspoon salt
2 cups cooked rice
1 cup grated cheddar cheese
6 slices bacon, cooked until crisp and crumbled

Combine flour, salt and anise seed. Cut butter and ½ cup cheese into mixture. (This step can be done in a food processor.) Press dough onto bottom and sides of an 8-inch springform or quiche pan. Preheat oven to 350°. Cook onion and garlic in bacon drippings over medium heat until soft. Add zucchini; continue to cook until wilted, stirring often. Combine eggs, sour cream, salt, rice and cheese. Add zucchini and bacon. Spoon into pastry shell. Bake 50 to 55 minutes or until center is firm. Cool; remove sides from springform pan. Cut into wedges before serving. Makes 6 servings.

BREADS

Baking Powder Biscuits

2 cups sifted all-purpose flour
3 teaspoons baking powder
½ teaspoon salt
6 tablespoons butter or shortening
¾ cup milk

Preheat oven to 450°. In a bowl, sift flour with the baking powder and salt. Cut in the butter or shortening (or a combination of the two) until the mixture resembles coarse meal. Stir the milk into the mixture until the dough forms a ball. Turn dough onto lightly floured surface and knead several times. Roll with floured rolling pin to a ½-inch thickness. Cut with biscuit cutter or small glass. Place on ungreased cookie sheet. Bake for 10 to 15 minutes, or until lightly browned. Makes 12 two-inch biscuits.

Cornmeal Biscuits

1½ cups sifted all-purpose flour
¾ cup cornmeal
¼ teaspoon baking soda
3 teaspoons baking powder
1 teaspoon salt
1 tablespoon sugar
4 tablespoons butter
1 egg, beaten
½ cup buttermilk or sour milk
Butter

Preheat oven to 450°. Sift dry ingredients together. Cut in the butter. Mix egg with buttermilk; add to dry ingredients. Turn onto floured board and knead lightly. Roll out to a ½-inch thickness. Cut with a biscuit cutter. Brush with butter and fold over into half-moon shape. Bake for 12 to 15 minutes or until golden. Makes 24 biscuits.

ANGEL BISCUITS

1 cup buttermilk
1 package dry yeast
1 teaspoon sugar
2½ cups all-purpose flour
1 teaspoon baking soda
1 teaspoon salt
¼ cup solid shortening
¼ cup butter, chilled
Flour
2 tablespoons butter, melted

Heat buttermilk to lukewarm, remove from heat and stir in yeast and sugar. Stir together flour, soda and salt. Cut shortening and butter into flour mixture with a pastry blender or two knives until it resembles coarse crumbs. Stir in buttermilk and yeast until well combined. Set aside for 10 minutes in refrigerator. Turn onto floured surface and knead several minutes. Roll out to a ½-inch thickness; cut with a biscuit cutter. Dip biscuits in melted butter and place on a baking sheet. Set aside to rise in a warm (85°) draft-free area until doubled in size. Preheat oven to 400°. Bake for 10 to 12 minutes or until lightly browned. Makes 16 to 20 biscuits.

ICEBOX ROLLS

2 packages dry yeast
¼ cup warm water (105° to 115°)
1 tablespoon sugar
1 cup boiling water
¾ cup solid shortening
¾ cup cold water
¼ cup sugar
1 teaspoon salt
2 eggs, beaten
6 cups all-purpose flour
Melted butter

Dissolve yeast and 1 tablespoon sugar in warm water. Set aside. In a large bowl stir boiling water into shortening to melt. When completely melted, add cold water, ¼ cup sugar and salt. Add eggs and yeast mixture; blend well. Gradually add flour, mixing well. Cover and chill for 24 hours. Turn dough out onto a lightly floured surface; knead for 2 to 3 minutes. Shape dough into 1½-inch balls; dip in melted butter and place on greased baking sheets. Set aside in a warm (85°) draft-free area for 1 hour or until doubled in size. Preheat oven to 400°. Bake for 12 to 15 minutes. Makes 3 dozen rolls.

GEORGIA PEACH MUFFINS

⅓ cup butter, melted
2 cups sour cream
2 eggs, beaten
4 cups all-purpose flour
⅔ cup firmly packed light brown sugar
2 tablespoons baking powder
1 teaspoon salt
½ teaspoon baking soda
¼ teaspoon cinnamon
¼ teaspoon nutmeg
3 medium peaches, peeled, pitted and chopped
¾ cup chopped pecans
Brown sugar

Preheat oven to 400°. Beat together butter, sour cream and eggs. Combine flour, sugar, baking powder, salt, soda and spices. Blend the dry ingredients into the sour cream mixture just until moistened (batter will be lumpy). Fold in the peaches and nuts. Spoon into paper-lined muffin cups, filling each about ⅔ full. Sprinkle the top of each muffin with a little brown sugar. Bake for 20 to 25 minutes or until golden brown. Serve warm. Makes 20 muffins.

SURPRISING SQUASH MUFFINS

1 cup cooked yellow squash
½ cup brown sugar
¼ cup sugar
¼ cup molasses
½ cup butter, softened
1 egg, beaten
1¾ cups all-purpose flour
1 teaspoon baking soda
¼ teaspoon salt
½ cup chopped nuts

Preheat oven to 375°. Mash and drain cooked squash. Set aside. Combine sugars, molasses and butter; add egg and squash. Blend well. Stir dry ingredients together; add to squash mixture. Add nuts; stir just until combined. Do not overmix. Fill well-greased muffin pans about half full with batter. Bake for 20 to 25 minutes or until a tester inserted in center comes out clean. Makes 18 muffins.

SOUTH OF THE MASON-DIXON LINE CORNBREAD

4 tablespoons bacon drippings or vegetable oil
1½ cups white cornmeal
½ cup all-purpose flour
1 teaspoon baking powder
1 teaspoon salt
½ teaspoon baking soda
2 eggs, beaten
1 cup buttermilk

Preheat oven to 425°. Melt bacon drippings in a 9-inch cast-iron skillet in the oven. Combine cornmeal, flour, baking powder, salt and soda. Whisk eggs into buttermilk; add to the cornmeal mixture, stirring just until blended. Pour hot drippings from skillet into batter; blend well. Pour batter into hot skillet. Bake for 20 to 25 minutes or until cornbread is golden brown. Cut into wedges to serve. Makes 8 servings.

Sweet Potato Muffin Delights

1¾ cups sifted all-purpose flour
1 teaspoon salt
3 teaspoons baking powder
2 tablespoons brown sugar
½ cup chopped walnuts
2 eggs, beaten
½ cup milk
¼ cup Jack Daniel's Whiskey
1¼ cups cooked and mashed sweet potatoes
¼ cup butter, melted
Cinnamon sugar

Preheat oven to 425°. Sift flour, salt and baking powder together. Stir in brown sugar and nuts. Combine eggs, milk, Jack Daniel's Whiskey, sweet potatoes and butter; mix well. Add potato mixture, all at once, to dry ingredients; mix only until ingredients are combined. Spoon into greased muffin tins. Sprinkle with cinnamon sugar. Bake for 35 to 40 minutes or until a tester inserted in center comes out clean. Makes 12 muffins.

Dog Bread

1 cup white cornmeal
¼ teaspoon salt
1 cup cold water
Bacon drippings

Stir together cornmeal and salt. Slowly add cold water. Set batter aside for 5 minutes. Using a heavy skillet, add bacon drippings until ⅛-inch deep. Drop batter by the spoonful into hot grease, allowing room to spread. Turn patties when golden and crisp and brown on one side. Remove when both sides are done. Drain on paper towels. Serve hot with butter. Makes 8 to 10 servings. Makes 2 dozen.

Hushpuppies

2 cups white cornmeal
¼ cup all-purpose flour
1 teaspoon baking powder
½ teaspoon baking soda
½ teaspoon salt
½ teaspoon pepper
3 tablespoons brown sugar
½ cup finely chopped onion
¼ cup finely chopped green pepper
½ cup buttermilk
⅔ cup water
½ cup bacon drippings or butter
1 egg, beaten
Vegetable oil

Combine dry ingredients with onion and green pepper. Combine buttermilk, water, bacon drippings and egg; stir into cornmeal mixture. Drop by spoonsful into hot oil (375°). You can use oil that has been used for fish. Fry until golden brown. Drain on paper towels. Makes 2½ dozen.

CORN MELBA TOAST

These are a little time consuming to make but are so delicious they will become a family favorite.

2 cups sifted all-purpose flour
2 teaspoons baking powder
1 teaspoon salt
½ cup butter, at room temperature
2 tablespoons sugar
2 large eggs
1 cup milk
1 cup water
½ cup white cornmeal

Preheat oven to 375°. Sift together flour, baking powder and salt. In a mixer, cream butter and sugar. Add eggs, one at a time, beating well after each addition. Scrape sides of bowl down with spatula. Combine milk and water. Alternately add dry ingredients and milk mixture to eggs in mixer ⅓ at a time. Add cornmeal and mix until smooth.

Spread batter into a 10½x15½x1-inch buttered jelly-roll pan. (You can bake more than one at a time if you have several pans, but swap shelves during baking and watch carefully.)

Measure ¾ cup plus 1 tablespoon batter for each pan. Pour along one short end of pan; scrape out the cup. Tilt pan so batter covers entire pan with a very thin coating (turning pan in all directions as needed). Bake for 5 minutes or until just firm enough to cut. Remove pan from oven. With a sharp knife cut into 16 rectangles. Return pan to oven and bake 15 to 20 minutes longer or until toast is lightly browned. Toast will not cook evenly. Remove each piece from pan with a spatula as they are done. Cool before storing in an airtight container (if they last that long). Makes 96.

LEMON CRACKERS

1 cup sugar, divided
1 teaspoon grated lemon rind
3 cups all-purpose flour
1 teaspoon baking powder
½ teaspoon salt
1 cup butter
2 eggs (1 separated)
¼ cup Jack Daniel's Whiskey, divided

Preheat oven to 375°. Mix ¼ cup sugar with lemon rind; set aside. Combine flour, ¾ cup sugar, baking powder and salt in bowl; stir lightly. Cut in butter with pastry cutter (food processor with steel blade may be used for this step). Beat one egg and one egg yolk with 3 tablespoons Jack Daniel's Whiskey. Stir into flour mixture until well blended. Chill dough for several hours. Roll out between sheets of waxed paper to a ⅛-inch thickness. Cut into 2-inch squares. Beat egg white with 1 tablespoon Jack Daniel's Whiskey until foamy. Brush over each cracker; sprinkle with lemon sugar mixture. Bake on ungreased cookie sheets for 8 to 10 minutes. Makes 6 dozen.

DOWN IN THE HOLLOW FRENCH TOAST

2 eggs, beaten
2 teaspoons sugar
⅛ teaspoon salt
¼ cup milk
1 tablespoon Jack Daniel's Whiskey
4 slices French bread, 1-inch thick
Butter
Confectioners' sugar or maple syrup

Beat together eggs, sugar, salt and milk. Stir in Jack Daniel's Whiskey. Dip bread slices in mixture. Melt butter in hot skillet. Brown each side of bread. Serve hot, sprinkled with confectioners' sugar or maple syrup. Makes 4 servings.

Moore County, Yesterday and Today

I f a portrait of the people in Moore County, Tennessee, could be painted, then the canvas framework would be built with belief—belief in self, in the land, in their fellowman and in their labor. The dominant color would be belief in the goodness of God.

The canvas would be woven with a variety of cultures; the fibers roughed by hard times, smoothed by good times and stretched taut by community effort.

The faces in the portrait would reflect strength of character, kindness, humor, laughter, honesty, love and caring. The texture would be etched deeply with failure and success.

Even if all this were done, the portrait would be incomplete because the people are so much more!

Like all Tennesseans the people of Moore County are proud of their heritage. Tennessee is called the Volunteer State because Tennesseans were the first to respond to defend their country in the War of 1812. From frontiersmen like Davy Crockett to soldiers like Sam Houston and Alvin York, they have fought bravely in battle. Statesmen and presidents have risen from these hills as surely as the mists on the mountains.

Moore County is the smallest county in the state, but it is as steeped in tradition as the rest. Lynchburg, the largest town and the county seat, has a population of fewer than 500. A farming community, the one big industry in town is whiskey making, and the people are proud of it. When Jack Daniel's Whiskey won a gold medal at the St. Louis World's Fair, everyone in the county felt that he had a part in winning.

Moore Countians are proud of their beginnings and of their contributions to the state and to the world. Their hometown product is sold in 100 countries around the world. They are proud of their rich agricultural heritage. However, when asked, they would tell you right off that their most valued treasure is the people—their friends and neighbors.

AUNTIE BLOSSOM'S CORNMEAL WAFFLES

1 egg
1½ cups milk
1½ cups self-rising cornmeal
¼ cup vegetable oil

Preheat waffle iron. Beat egg, then add remaining ingredients; stir vigorously until smooth. Bake in waffle iron until golden brown. Serve hot with butter and syrup *or* these make a perfect base for chicken á la king!

GERMAN APPLE PANCAKE

3 tablespoons butter, divided
3 eggs
½ cup milk
¼ cup all-purpose flour
3 tablespoons sugar, divided
½ teaspoon salt
1 large cooking apple, peeled, cored and sliced
¼ teaspoon cinnamon

Preheat oven to 450°. In oven, melt 1 tablespoon butter in 9-inch pie plate. Tilt plate so butter completely covers bottom. Set aside. Beat eggs,

milk, flour, 1 tablespoon sugar and salt until smooth. Pour into hot pie plate; bake for 8 minutes. Reduce heat to 375°. Bake until golden brown and sides are puffy, about 8 minutes longer. Meanwhile, in saucepan, combine apple slices, remaining butter and sugar and cinnamon. Cook over low heat, stirring until tender, about 10 minutes. Spoon apple mixture over hot pancake. Serve immediately. Makes 1 to 2 servings.

BANANA FRITTERS

    1 cup sifted all-purpose flour
    1 tablespoon sugar
    1 teaspoon baking powder
    ½ teaspoon salt
    1 large egg, beaten
    ¾ cup milk
    1 tablespoon butter, melted
    6 bananas, each cut in 3 or 4 diagonal pieces
    Peanut oil
    Honey Butter

In medium bowl, sift together flour, sugar, baking powder and salt. Combine the egg, milk and butter. Stir liquid into dry ingredients. If possible, set batter aside, covered, in refrigerator for several hours or overnight (this breaks down rubberiness). Preheat oil in deep fryer to 375°. Dip banana pieces in batter and drop into hot oil. Fry until golden brown. Serve hot with Honey Butter. Makes 6 servings.

HONEY BUTTER

    ½ cup honey
    ½ cup butter, softened
    1 teaspoon grated orange rind

Beat honey into butter. Add orange rind and continue beating until light and fluffy. Makes 1 cup.

MR. JACK'S SPOON BREAD

    2 cups milk, heated
    1 cup cornmeal
    ½ cup butter
    ½ teaspoon salt
    1 tablespoon sugar
    4 eggs, separated
    2 tablespoons Jack Daniel's Whiskey

Preheat oven to 350°. Grease a 1½-quart baking dish. In a saucepan, stir cornmeal into heated milk and cook until thickened. Remove from heat; add butter, salt and sugar. Stir until butter melts; set aside. Stir beaten egg yolks into cornmeal mixture. Beat egg whites until stiff; fold into cornmeal mixture. Stir in Jack Daniel's Whiskey. Pour batter into baking dish. Bake for 40 minutes or until slightly brown and crusty on top. Makes 8 servings.

ALBERTA'S APRICOT LOAF

    1 cup chopped dried apricots
    ¼ cup boiling water
    2½ cups sifted all-purpose flour
    1 cup sugar
    ¼ teaspoon salt
    ¼ teaspoon baking powder
    ¼ teaspoon baking soda
    2 eggs, beaten
    1 cup buttermilk
    ¼ cup apricot nectar
    3 tablespoons butter, melted
    1 cup chopped walnuts

Preheat oven to 350°. Soak apricots in boiling water. Set aside. Sift together flour, sugar, salt, baking powder and baking soda. Stir together eggs, buttermilk, nectar and melted butter. Drain apricots. Add buttermilk mixture to dry ingredients along with chopped apricots and nuts. Pour into greased loaf pan. Bake for 1 hour or until tester inserted in center comes out clean. Makes 1 loaf.

LADIES OF LYNCHBURG TEA LOAF

>   3 cups all-purpose flour, unsifted
>   1 cup sugar
>   4 teaspoons baking powder
> 1½ teaspoons salt
>   ¼ cup butter
>   2 teaspoons grated orange rind
> 1¾ cups chopped pecans, divided
>   1 egg
>   1 cup milk
>   ½ cup Jack Daniel's Whiskey

Preheat oven to 350°. Grease and flour 9x5x3-inch loaf pan. In bowl, combine flour, sugar, baking powder and salt. Cut in butter until mixture resembles coarse crumbs (this can be done in a food processor). Add grated orange rind and 1½ cups chopped pecans. In small bowl, combine egg, milk and Jack Daniel's Whiskey. Add liquid to dry ingredients just until blended. Turn into loaf pan. Sprinkle ¼ cup chopped pecans over top. Bake 1 hour or until tester inserted in center comes out clean. Cool in pan 10 minutes. Turn onto rack to cool completely. Makes 18 ½-inch-thick slices.

BUSY DAY CASSEROLE BREAD

>   1 cup small curd cottage cheese
>   1 package dry yeast
>   ¼ cup warm water
>   2 tablespoons sugar
>   1 tablespoon butter
>   2 tablespoons dill seed
>   1 teaspoon salt
>   ¼ teaspoon baking soda
>   1 unbeaten egg
> 2½ cups all-purpose flour

Heat cheese until lukewarm. Dissolve yeast in warm water and combine with cheese. Add remaining ingredients. Knead for a few minutes on floured board or plate. Place into a greased 2-quart casserole. Set aside to rise until doubled in size. Punch down and let rise again until doubled in size. Preheat oven to 350°. Bake for 30 minutes. This is good spread with garlic butter and toasted. Makes 1 large loaf.

BANANA RAISIN BREAD
(For Adults Only)

>   ¼ cup Jack Daniel's Whiskey
>   1 cup raisins
>   2 cups all-purpose flour
>   1 teaspoon baking soda
>   ½ teaspoon salt
>   1 cup sugar
>   ½ cup butter
>   2 eggs
>   3 medium bananas, thinly sliced
>   1 teaspoon vanilla
>   ½ cup pecans

Preheat oven to 325°. Plump raisins by soaking in Jack Daniel's Whiskey. Sift together flour, soda, and salt. Cream sugar and butter. Beat in eggs. Add raisins, Jack Daniel's Whiskey, bananas and vanilla. Stir in dry ingredients and pecans. Pour the batter into a greased 9x5x3-inch loaf pan. Bake for 1 hour or until tester inserted in center comes out clean. Makes 1 loaf.

BACON CHEESE BREAD

>   4 slices bacon
>   ¼ cup chopped green onion
>   2 tablespoons chopped fresh parsley
>   2 cups all-purpose flour, unsifted
>   2 teaspoons baking powder
>   2 teaspoons dry mustard
>   ½ teaspoon salt
>   1 cup milk
>   2 eggs, beaten
>   1 cup grated Jarlsberg cheese

Preheat oven to 375°. Cook bacon slices until crisp; remove from skillet and crumble. Add onion and parsley to drippings. Cook until onion is tender. Remove skillet from heat. Stir together flour, baking powder, mustard and salt. Blend milk and eggs together. Add onion mixture with drippings, cheese, crumbled bacon and milk-egg mixture to dry ingredients all at once. Blend just until moistened. Pour batter into greased 9x5x3-inch loaf pan. Bake for 1 hour or until tester inserted in center comes out clean. Cool in pan 10 minutes. Invert onto wire rack. Makes 1 loaf.

WHISKEY NUT BREAD

8 eggs, separated
3 cups sugar, divided

1 pound butter
3 cups sifted all-purpose flour
½ cup Jack Daniel's Whiskey
2 teaspoons vanilla
2 teaspoons almond extract
1 cup chopped pecans

Preheat oven to 350°. Beat egg whites until soft peaks form. Gradually add 1 cup sugar, beating until stiff peaks form. Cream butter and remaining sugar. Add egg yolks, one at a time, beating well after each addition. Add flour, ⅓ cup at a time, alternating with Jack Daniel's Whiskey. Mix well. Stir in vanilla, almond extract and pecans. Fold in egg whites. Pour into 3 greased 9x5x3-inch loaf pans. Bake for 1 hour or until a tester inserted in center comes out clean. This freezes well. Makes 3 loaves.

LOAF BREAD

To shape loaves of bread: Roll ball of dough with a rolling pin into a 14x19-inch rectangle. Roll up the rectangle tightly from the narrow side pressing with your thumbs to seal the dough at each turn. Pinch edges and ends to seal. Fold ends under. Place the loaf in the pan and make sure that both ends touch the ends of the pan. This will assure a lovely uniform bread loaf.

MIZ SMITH'S LOAF BREAD

1½ cups water
1 cup milk
3 tablespoons sugar
2 packages yeast
7 cups all-purpose flour
1 tablespoon salt
¼ cup solid shortening
Butter

Heat water, milk and sugar until lukewarm. Remove from heat. Add yeast and stir vigorously. In a large bowl, combine flour, salt and shortening. Add milk mixture and mix for about 10 minutes (you can do this with a mixer). Set dough aside for 1 hour or until doubled in size. Punch down and divide into two loaves. Roll out with rolling pin forming two rectangles. Form into two loaves; place each in a well-greased 1-pound loaf pan. Set aside for 1 hour or until dough doubles in size. Preheat oven to 350°. Brush tops with melted butter. Bake for 50 minutes or until golden brown. Turn out on rack to cool. Makes 2 loaves.

COUNTRY LOAF BREAD

2 packages dry yeast
2 cups warm water (105° to 115°)
½ cup sugar, divided
2 eggs, beaten
¼ cup vegetable oil
1 teaspoon salt
6 cups all-purpose flour

Dissolve yeast in warm water; set aside for 5 minutes. Add 1 tablespoon sugar and stir. Whisk together remaining sugar, eggs, oil and salt. In a large bowl, combine yeast mixture, egg mixture and half the flour, mixing well. Gradually stir in remaining flour. Turn dough out onto lightly floured surface. Knead for 8 to 10 minutes or until smooth and elastic. Shape dough into a ball; place in a well-greased bowl, turning once to grease top. Cover and set aside to rise in a warm (85°) draft-free area until doubled in size 1½ to 2 hours.

Hint: When dough is properly risen, an imprint will remain when you press lightly with your fingers. Punch dough down; divide in half and place on a floured surface. Roll each half into a rectangular shape. Beginning at narrow edge, roll up dough; press firmly to eliminate air pockets. Place loaves, seam-side down into 2 well-greased 9x5x3-inch loaf pans. Brush tops lightly with oil. Cover loaves and set aside to rise again until almost doubled in size. Preheat oven to 375°. Bake on lower rack in oven for 30 to 35 minutes or until loaves sound hollow when tapped on bottom. Remove at once from pans. Cool on wire rack before storing. Makes 2 loaves.

DODIE'S SODA BREAD

3 cups all-purpose flour
¼ teaspoon baking soda
½ teaspoon salt
1 teaspoon baking powder

1 stick butter, softened
¾ cup raisins
1 egg
½ cup sugar
¾ cup buttermilk

In a large bowl, combine first 4 ingredients. Blend in butter; add raisins. Beat egg and sugar in separate bowl, then add the buttermilk. Pour into the flour and raisin mixture; mix well. Preheat oven to 450°. Knead for about 4 minutes. Shape dough into a round loaf and place in a lightly greased pie pan. Cut a large X on top with a knife. Bake for 45 minutes or until golden brown. Makes 1 round loaf.

. . . .

BATTER BREADS

Batter bread is beaten instead of kneaded. Yeast breads will need to rise twice, while batter bread will rise once, therefore, taking less time to make. Batter bread is open-textured with full old-fashioned home-baked flavor.

. . . .

OLD TIME GRAHAM CRACKER BREAD

⅔ cup sifted all-purpose flour
½ teaspoon salt
3 teaspoons baking powder
2 cups graham cracker crumbs
⅔ cup chopped pecans, optional
1 cup firmly packed brown sugar
¼ cup solid shortening, softened
1 teaspoon vanilla
2 eggs
⅔ cup milk

Sift flour, salt and baking powder into bowl. Add cracker crumbs, nuts and sugar; stir. Add shortening, vanilla, eggs and milk; mix well, quickly but thoroughly. Preheat oven to 375°. Place in a greased 6-cup loaf pan. Bake for 50 minutes or until bread begins to pull away from the sides of the pan. Turn out on rack to cool. Makes 1 loaf.

EASY TOMATO BREAD

2½ cups all-purpose flour
1 tablespoon baking powder
1 teaspoon salt
1 teaspoon garlic salt
1 teaspoon crushed dried oregano
1 tablespoon finely minced parsley
1 tablespoon sugar
½ cup shredded Mozzarella cheese
¼ cup grated Parmesan cheese
    Milk
1½ cups peeled, chopped canned tomatoes, drained (reserve liquid)
2 eggs
¼ cup vegetable oil

Preheat oven to 350°. Combine flour, baking powder, salts, oregano, parsley, sugar and cheeses. Add enough milk to drained tomato liquid to make ⅔ cup. Blend liquid with eggs and oil. Stir liquids and chopped tomatoes into flour mixture. Mix thoroughly. Pour batter into greased 9x5x3-inch loaf pan. Bake for 1 hour and 15 minutes. (A long baking time is required.) Remove to a wire rack; cool before cutting. Makes 1 loaf.

The Farmer's Produce Wagon

I n the early days of Tennessee, when settlements were few and only a handful of pioneers dotted the vast hillsides and rolling lands, horseback peddlers sold needles and pins, coffee and sugar, seeds and medicines to ladies too far afield to come to town to purchase wares. In addition to such goods, the peddlers brought the latest news from town and sometimes stayed the night. As the area became more populated and towns sprouted up, these peddlers were less necessary.

However, instead of buying goods carried from the town, many farmers found that they had a need to sell goods carried to the town. Farmers' markets in the big city were started and farm-to-market roads crisscrossed the countryside. Still, small farmers produced quality products in small quantities with not enough help to spend a day a week selling in a farmers' market. A little creative thinking brought about a reversal of the town peddler going out into the countryside to find a buyer. The farmer brought his specialty to the local community where townfolk had no time to homecure meats, churn butter, or make farm cheese. Mary Bobo, for instance, bought food for her boardinghouse from produce wagons that came to Lynchburg.

Small towns benefit from these small farmers' quality produce. Tennesseans take special pride in their sorghum, honey from their hives, homemade cheeses and their homecured country hams. Prized family recipes handed down for generations produce wonderful smoked sausages and country hams.

Farmers still bring their goods to town by wagon or truck and townfolk benefit greatly from this small business venture. Country ham, red eye gravy, grits, biscuits, and honey make about the best eating in the world. That's why when a farmer shows up with his wagon full of honey and hams, sausage and sorghum, townfolk gather quickly to make sure they get a part of this quality produce.

AUNT CASSIE'S CASSEROLE RYE BREAD

1 cup milk, scalded
¼ cup firmly packed brown sugar
1 teaspoon salt
¼ cup butter
2 packages dry yeast
1 cup warm water
2 tablespoons caraway seed
3 cups all-purpose flour
2 cups rye flour
   Milk
   Caraway seed

In a large bowl, pour scalded milk over brown sugar, salt and butter. Cool. Dissolve yeast in warm water; add to *cooled* milk mixture. Add caraway seed and half of each flour; blend with electric mixer (or food processor) on medium speed until smooth. Add remaining flour and beat until well blended. Cover bowl; place in a warm place to rise until doubled in size, about 45 minutes. Preheat oven to 350°. Punch down; stir vigorously for 30 seconds. Place into a well-buttered 2-quart casserole. Brush top with milk and sprinkle with caraway seed. Bake for 45 to 50 minutes. Turn out onto a rack to cool. Makes 1 loaf.

OVERNIGHT OATMEAL BREAD

½ cup quick-cooking oats, uncooked
1 cup boiling water
1 package yeast
⅓ cup warm water
¼ cup sorghum or molasses
1 tablespoon margarine
1¼ teaspoons salt
3 cups all-purpose flour, divided
   Vegetable oil

Combine oats and boiling water; set aside until cooled to warm. Dissolve yeast in warm water. When oat mixture is same temperature as yeast mixture, combine. Add sorghum, margarine and salt; blend well. Stir in 2 cups of flour and mix thoroughly. Knead in last cup of flour by hand, adding additional flour, if needed, to make a stiff dough. Set aside for 5 minutes. Meanwhile, grease a 1-pound loaf pan (a refrigerator-to-oven pan). Turn dough onto floured board; knead for 10 minutes. Shape into a loaf; place in prepared pan. Lightly oil top of loaf. Cover; place in refrigerator (at least 8 hours, or up to 24 hours). Remove from refrigerator 10 minutes to 1 hour before baking. Preheat oven to 350°. Bake for 50 minutes. Loaf is done when it sounds hollow when lightly tapped on bottom. Cool on rack. Makes 1 loaf.

ENTRÉES

MISS MARY'S FAMOUS CHICKEN WITH PASTRY

If there is one thing more famous in Miss Mary's Boarding House kitchen than this Famous Chicken with Pastry, it is the lady who prepares it and her singing. Velma Waggoner, the singing cook, as everyone refers to her, sings while she cooks. She will sing Christmas songs in summer and "Here comes Peter Cottontail" in February, all to the enjoyment of her co-workers.

1 2½ to 3-pound chicken
1 onion
1 rib celery
1 teaspoon salt
4 tablespoons all-purpose flour
  Salt and pepper to taste
2 cups all-purpose flour
1 teaspoon salt
¾ cup shortening (we use lard)
¼ cup cold water

Place chicken in 3 cups water with onion, celery and 1 teaspoon salt. Cook until tender over medium heat. When tender, remove chicken from broth and debone. Cut into large chunks and place in the bottom of a greased 9x12-inch baking dish. Remove celery and onion from broth. Blend 4 tablespoons flour with ¼ cup water and gradually whisk into simmering broth. Cook for 5 to 10 minutes or until thickened. Season with salt and pepper. Pour enough sauce over chicken to just cover. Preheat oven to 375°. Combine 2 cups flour and 1 teaspoon salt. Cut shortening into flour with a pastry blender or fork until mixture resembles cornmeal. Sprinkle with water; mix until it holds together and forms a ball. Roll out on floured board to about a ¼-inch thickness. Cut into strips and place over chicken. Bake until pastry has browned. Makes 4 servings.

Traditional Southern Fried Chicken

  1 2 to 2½ pound chicken, cut up
1½ cups all-purpose flour
1½ teaspoons salt
  1 teaspoon pepper
  3 cups vegetable oil

Shake chicken pieces in a bag with flour, salt and pepper. Set pieces aside to dry before frying. Heat oil in a heavy 10-inch skillet (cast iron is best) over medium high heat. When oil is quite hot, add thighs and legs, skin-side down. Cook for several minutes; then add other pieces. Continue cooking until chicken is golden brown on one side (about 5 minutes), turn over, and brown on the other side. Reduce heat to medium low. Cover the pan and cook for 15 minutes. Turn pieces, cover, continue to cook for 15 minutes longer. Uncover for the last 5 to 10 minutes so that crust will be crisp. Makes 4 servings.

Note: Old timers used bacon drippings to fry their chicken. You might want to add several tablespoons to the vegetable oil for flavor. The chicken at Miss Mary Bobo's Boarding House is fried in lard, which gives it that faintly sweetish taste that guests rave about.

Chicken Breasts Supreme

  2 chicken breasts, split and skinned
  2 tablespoons butter, divided
  4 slices country ham
  1 cup heavy cream
⅓ cup apple cider
  1 tablespoon lemon juice
    Salt and pepper to taste
  4 slices buttered toast

Sauté chicken breasts in 1 tablespoon butter over medium heat, 6 to 8 minutes per side. Add the ham slices and heat through. Add cream and bring to a boil. Remove chicken and ham from skillet and keep in a warm oven while finishing sauce. Reduce the cream by half and add cider. Simmer 1 minute. Whisk in 1 tablespoon butter and lemon juice. Season with salt and pepper. To serve, top each slice of toast with a slice of ham and chicken. Divide sauce over each. Makes 4 servings.

Hog Killing Time in Tennessee

······································

The Way It Was Done When I Was a Lad

by Erskine H. Early

Recipes for doing things have been exchanged since time began. A person finds a new way to make something, preserve something, or do something, and the first thing you know, he's talking to his neighbor about it. It was this same spirit of sharing that caused early settlers to help each other build barns, cut timber, stitch a quilt, harvests crops or raise a roof—any job that was too big for one person to do by himself.

But shared work was more than just a way to get things done. It was a way of getting together with your neighbors. In Tennessee folks got together for barn raisings, sorghum stir-offs or tobacco hangings. Erskine Early of Spring Hill, Tennessee, shares a childhood remembrance of hog killing. It's an insight into how neighbors worked together, preserving our country at its finest. This is the kind of occasion we all like to reminisce about from time to time. Well-flavored and spiced with homespun humor, this could be titled "Country Preserves."

Hog killing time—especially to a hill country lad—was one of the most exciting times of the year. For one thing, I got to miss school that day. Coming as it did in late fall, it was the last big event on the farm before the onset of the winter doldrums. It might aptly be called the country fellows' Mardi Gras. Except for the all too short glitter and excitement of Christmas, the rest of the long winter was mighty dull. Each man

"swapped work" by helping his neighbor butcher. It took many strong backs to heft a 500-pound hog. There was the promise of plenty of fresh meat for the table—fried back strip, savory, tangy country sausage, liver, souse and all the delicious fixin's Mom would make. And, too, there were the unexplainable thrills that only a country lad of 10 or 12 years of age can experience.

Suitable weather for killing usually came in late November or early December. As the days grew shorter and the cold breath of winter rode the brisk north wind, you would hear the menfolk exclaim, "That wind is coming through the peach orchard this morning. . . . It's going to be hog killing weather before long." (As a boy, I never did figure out why wind "coming through the peach orchard" was colder than wind coming through anything else. It was just something you accepted as fact and didn't show your ignorance by asking why.) Then would come the day when, as the winter sun slowly sank behind the western hills, Dad would check his weather signs and announce, "We will kill hogs tomorrow."

Down near the creek and spring house, the big wooden scalder with its metal bottom would be in place over the fire pit, the gangling poles would be up and plenty of firewood stacked nearby. Next morning, Dad and we boys would be up by at least 4 o'clock. Fortified with a huge country breakfast and bundled against the cold, we would tote water from the creek and fill the scalder. With a roaring wood fire under it, soon great clouds of steam would tower into the still, frosty cold, morning air. As the first rays of the morning sun turned the frost on the rail fence to diamonds, the neighbors who were going to help would be arriving. Each would bring his own knife—usually handmade and tempered and honed razor sharp—in which he took great pride. Everyone was skillful at his job, and with many hands making small work, the whole job was usually completed in plenty of time for everyone to get home and do chores before sunset. Huge cups of steaming hot coffee brought by the womenfolk helped things along. I wasn't big enough to help much with the heavy work, and so I would stand by the scalder fire trying to keep warm. Even now I can feel my front side burning up while it felt as if my hind side was turning blue with frostbite! A large pan of hot biscuits together with fried pork cooked in a big iron skillet over hot coals dragged from the scalder fire was lunch—all washed down with strong, hot coffee. This was one time of the year the womenfolk didn't have time to fix a big dinner for the hands.

Cut into its various pieces, the meat was placed in some vacant building to chill overnight. The next day, the meat would be trimmed and packed down. Uncle Charlie Ward, who was part Cherokee and the best meat trimmer in the country, always helped with this job. To Uncle Charlie, trimming a ham was a work of art. No sculptor ever took more pains with his work. The meat was then hand rubbed with salt and placed on the salt-covered bottom of the meat box. Covered with more salt—being careful to fill the cracks and crevices—this process was repeated until all the meat was packed down. Here it would stay for three to six weeks.

The big job the next day was lard rendering. All the hog fat would be cut into small pieces and placed in a huge cast-iron rendering kettle and cooked over a fire out in the yard. When the pieces of fat turned to brown cracklin's, the lard was put in fifty-pound tin "stands." The cracklin's were carefully saved to be used in making cracklin' bread that, made according to our family recipe, is a never-to-be-forgotten treat.

Then there was the sausage! We saved all the very best, lean trimmings for sausage. We made our own seasoning—and we still do. It is a special blend of peppers, sage and other natural spices that we have kept a secret for forty years, and no one has ever successfully copied it. Ground and seasoned just right and sizzling in the skillet, you can smell that delicious aroma a half mile down wind. We ate some fresh, but the way we like it best is to pack it in cloth pokes and slow smoke it many days over a smoldering green, hickory wood fire until it turns a golden brown. I still make and smoke sausage this same way, and I have never grown tired of its real country-smoked flavor.

Now to get back to the meat we packed down in the cure. In about three or four weeks the meat was ready to "come up." Removed from the salt and thoroughly washed, it was hung in the smokehouse for smoking and aging. We used then, as now, green hickory wood chips and sawdust. We kept a slow, smoldering smoke fire going for up to six weeks until the meat was a golden brown. The pokes of sausage were smoked for only a week or ten days. The mouth-watering smell of Dad's country-smoked sausage would make any sleepyhead come bounding out of bed onto the cold floor, wide awake! And, of course, that went for the smoked hams and lean streaked bacon, too.

In a way, it is sad that hog killing time is almost a thing of the past. To be able to grow and preserve your own meat supply for a whole year imparted a feeling of pride, self-reliance and independence that is so often lacking in this modern age. Sure, it took long hours and hard work. But, to me at least, it was worth it!

INTOXICATED CHICKEN

1 2½ to 3-pound chicken, cut into pieces, or 4 chicken
    breasts
    Salt and pepper to taste
2 tablespoons butter
2 tablespoons vegetable oil
½ cup Jack Daniel's Whiskey
6 shallots, chopped or 1 onion, chopped
¼ teaspoon powdered thyme
¼ cup minced fresh parsley
¼ cup water
1 cup heavy cream

Sprinkle chicken with salt and pepper. In a large skillet, heat the butter and oil; brown the chicken pieces on both sides. Add the Jack Daniel's Whiskey and carefully ignite, shaking the skillet until the flames go out. Add the shallots and cook for 1 minute. Add the thyme, parsley and water; cover skillet and cook over low heat, turning occasionally, 25 to 35 minutes. Transfer chicken to warm platter. Add the cream to the skillet and simmer, stirring until sauce thickens. Serve sauce over chicken. Makes 4 servings.

BAKED DOVE

10 doves, cleaned
    Salt and pepper to taste
3 apples, cored and sliced
2 onions, sliced
10 slices bacon, halved
1 cup chicken broth

Preheat oven to 325°. Sprinkle doves with salt and pepper. Arrange apple slices in bottom of a greased 6x10-inch casserole. Top each apple slice with an onion slice. Wrap doves with bacon, being careful to cover entire breast. Place doves atop onion. Pour broth into dish; cover. Bake 1 hour or until doves are tender. Remove cover during last 15 minutes of cooking. Makes 3 to 4 servings.

BAKED TURKEY WITH CORNBREAD DRESSING

1 10 to 12-pound turkey
¼ cup butter, softened
1 onion
1 rib celery

Preheat oven to 350°. Remove giblets, rinse turkey and pat dry. Sprinkle cavity with salt and rub outside with softened butter. Place onion and celery inside cavity. Place in roaster; cover and cook 20 minutes per pound, about 3 to 3½ hours. After baking, discard onion and celery and reserve broth for dressing. Makes 10 to 12 servings.

CORNBREAD DRESSING

3 eggs
3 cups self-rising cornmeal
2 cups buttermilk
½ cup vegetable oil or bacon drippings
½ cup chopped celery
½ cup chopped onion
1 tablespoon sage
2 teaspoons black pepper
2 to 3 cups turkey broth

Preheat oven to 425°. Mix the first four ingredients together and pour into a well greased 12-inch skillet. Bake for 20 minutes until golden brown. Crumble cornbread into a large bowl. Add celery, onion, sage and black pepper to crumbled cornbread. Stir in 2 or more cups of broth from turkey or just enough to moisten. Pour into well-greased 9x13-inch glass dish and bake until golden brown, about 35 to 40 minutes. Makes 10 to 12 servings.

Sprinkle gelatin over ¼ cup Jack Daniel's Whiskey to soften. Dissolve over heat. Melt butter; add flour and stir over low heat several minutes. Slowly add heated milk; stir until smooth and thick. Add remaining Jack Daniel's Whiskey and nutmeg. Blend egg yolks with heavy cream; stir in small amount of hot sauce, then add mixture to sauce. Stir over low heat until well thickened; add gelatin, ham, dash of cayenne pepper and salt to taste. Rinse a mold with cold water. Pour in mixture; chill until mousse is firm. Unmold and garnish with sliced hard-boiled eggs and gherkins. Makes 6 servings.

TENNESSEE BAKED HAM IN A BLANKET

Some winters it gets so cold in Lynchburg that everyone goes under cover. Snow blankets the ground and heavy coats and tarps are brought out to cover man and beast. The other day we had a real winter storm, and Mayor Nath Osborn was quoted as saying, "Lynchburg was colder than Hell." As it turned out, he was right. Lynchburg's temperature was six degrees colder than the temperature recorded in Hell, Michigan!

Here's a recipe that features a blanket which will add spirit and spice to baked ham and is guaranteed to please any time of the year.

1 6-pound ham
4 cups all-purpose flour
1 cup dark brown sugar
2 tablespoons each: cinnamon, ground cloves, dry mustard
1 teaspoon fresh cracked pepper
Enough Jack Daniel's Whiskey to make a stiff dough

Prepare ham for baking by removing excess fat and any skin. Combine remaining ingredients to make a stiff dough. Roll dough out on a bread board. Form into a square large enough to wrap the ham. If you roll dough out onto a sheet of aluminum foil, wrap ham in pastry and foil. Place ham in cold oven. Turn thermostat to 325° and bake according to time

HAM MOUSSE

1 tablespoon unflavored gelatin
½ cup Jack Daniel's Whiskey, divided
¼ cup butter
¼ cup all-purpose flour
1 cup milk, heated
½ teaspoon nutmeg
2 egg yolks
½ cup heavy cream
2 cups finely chopped cooked ham
    Cayenne pepper
    Salt
    Hard-boiled eggs, sliced
    Sweet gherkins

100

chart on ham label. Remove from oven; cool ham for 20 minutes. Remove foil and slice. Makes 12 to 16 servings.

PORK ROAST

   1 4 to 5-pound pork loin roast
   1 teaspoon vinegar
   1 tablespoon brown sugar
   2 teaspoons all-purpose flour
   1 teaspoon paprika
   ½ teaspoon salt
   ½ teaspoon pepper
   ¼ cup Jack Daniel's Whiskey
   ¼ cup water
   1 bay leaf
   2 tablespoons parsley, minced

Rub roast with vinegar. Combine brown sugar, flour, paprika, salt and pepper; rub over entire roast. Place roast on rack, fat-side up, in baking pan. Set roast aside for 1 hour. Preheat oven to 450°. Pour Jack Daniel's Whiskey and water in bottom of pan. Add bay leaf to liquid. Sprinkle parsley over roast. Reduce oven heat at once to 325°. Cook roast, uncovered, for 25 to 35 minutes per pound (internal temperature when done should be 170°). Baste frequently during cooking. Remove roast from oven and set aside for 15 minutes before carving. Makes 6 to 8 servings.

PORK CHOPS WITH APRICOT STUFFING

   ½ pound mushrooms
   ⅓ cup chopped onion
   ⅓ cup chopped celery
   ½ cup butter, divided
   ½ cup dried apricots
   1 cup bread crumbs
   ¼ teaspoon ground sage
   ½ cup chopped parsley

   4 1-inch thick double loin pork chops
   Salt and pepper to taste
   1 cup dry white wine or chicken stock

Preheat oven to 350°. Reserve 4 mushrooms for garnish; slice remainder. Sauté mushrooms, onion and celery in ¼ cup butter until tender. Reserve 4 apricots; chop remainder and add to mushroom mixture along with bread crumbs, sage and parsley. Set aside. Trim off excess fat and cut a large pocket in the side of each chop. Sprinkle chops inside and out with salt and pepper. Fill the pockets with stuffing. Secure openings with toothpicks. Brown chops in ovenproof dish on both sides in remaining ¼ cup butter. Pour wine around chops. Cover. Bake for 1 hour or until tender. Garnish with reserved mushrooms and apricots. Makes 4 servings.

FLAMING TENNESSEE TENDERLOIN

   2 pounds pork tenderloin
   Juice of 1 large orange
   4 cloves garlic, crushed
   2 teaspoons grated fresh ginger or ¼ teaspoon
      ground ginger
   3 tablespoons soy sauce
   1 tablespoon brown sugar
   1 tablespoon toasted sesame seeds
   ⅓ cup Jack Daniel's Whiskey

Preheat oven to 350°. Trim tenderloin. Combine all remaining ingredients except Jack Daniel's Whiskey. Marinate pork overnight. To cook, remove from marinade and place on rack in roasting pan. Bake in moderate oven until pork is done. Allow 30 minutes per pound and baste with marinade every 10 minutes. Remove from oven, slice tenderloin and arrange on flameproof serving platter. Warm Jack Daniel's Whiskey and carefully ignite; pour over meat. Serve at the table while still flaming. Makes 4 to 6 servings.

The Hunt, The Hunter, The Hound

Hunting just seems to be in the blood of the people here in Tennessee. And stories of the hunt are always the cream of fireside stories. They beat fish stories by a country mile. When you go out to fish, well, you catch one or you don't. But with hunting, almost anything can and does—to believe the stories—happen.

Every hunter has his hound dog. Yarns and tales about the hounds satisfy the moments when the hunters rest.

In this part of the country, no one goes out to hunt bear. But stories are told right regular of how while hunting for rabbit or coons, there is a chance meeting with a bear! A rabbit gun's sure no arm against a bear, no matter what his size. If the hunter is able to think at all, then he prays hard that the big one on this trip will get away—and without his hide in tow.

It's at this point, invariably, that the feats of the hound dog are revealed. The complete devotion to his calling, not to mention that same all-encompassing devotion to his master, riles him to his greatest moment. His hair bristles, his teeth are bared, a snarl so deep and fearful it sets the heart to pounding and knees to quaking breaks the stillness of the moment. He crouches low before he springs at the assailant.

At this instant the bear, realizing that he has come upon man's most esteemed protector, unrestrained in the moment and hell-bent on victory in his charge, decides that he does not wish to suffer defeat, turns tail and runs! The hound, undaunted, is at his heels, barking, yapping to remind the bear of his dishonor.

Only by the fireside after the hunt does the valor and humor of the situation unfold as the hunter proclaims the victory of his favorite hound; his courage is expounded. The exalted hound, to everyone's amazement, lolls unperturbed upon the floor. He is as he was before the hunt, devoted to his master and to his calling, nothing more.

HOW TO COOK COUNTRY HAM

Boiling Country Ham. Cut off hock, clean whole ham thoroughly with a brush and rough cloth. Trim off any dark, dry edges and discolored fat. Since the hams have a dry cure, soaking in water around 8 hours before cooking is often desirable. Use fresh water for cooking. Fill large roaster about ½ full with water. Place ham on rack skin-side up. Start ham cooking at high heat, when water boils reduce heat to simmer and continue cooking until ham is tender. Cook approximately 30 minutes per pound or until meat thermometer registers 160 degrees. One tablespoon of brown sugar or molasses per quart of water may be added; ¼ cup vinegar or red wine may be added to the water if desired. Allow ham to cool in the juice 4 or 5 hours; this will bring the internal temperature to 170 degrees. Remove from broth and skin ham. Use your favorite glaze.

Baking Country Ham. Prepare as for boiling. Place ham, skin-side up, on a rack in an open pan. Start ham covered or in aluminum foil in a 375 degree oven for 1 hour. Reduce heat to 200 to 225 degrees and cook until the center of the ham registers 160 degrees on a meat thermometer. This will take about 45 to 50 minutes per pound for whole hams. Hams continue to cook after removal from oven. For well done meat, internal temperature should reach 170 degrees. Remove skin and allow ham to cool slightly. Either serve as is or glaze.

Note. Baked hams are much easier to slice when chilled. Cut slices thin and perpendicular to the bone.

To glaze baked or boiled ham: After ham is cooked, remove skin with sharp knife, score, cover with glaze, stick cloves about every inch and bake at 350 to 400 degrees for about 30 minutes or until

lightly browned. Glaze may be made of combinations of brown sugar and fruit juice, crushed pineapple or honey. Serve hot or cold.

Fried Country Ham. Skin should only be removed from the area where the slices will be taken. Cut ham slices ¼ to ⅜-inch thick. Do not trim any excess fat from the slices until after frying. Use a heavy skillet that will distribute heat evenly. Fat edges should be scored to prevent curling. Place slices in skillet with fat edges toward the center. Do not cover, fry slowly at medium heat. Turn frequently. Do not over-fry or cook on high heat; grease should not splatter. Cook until both sides of ham are very lightly browned. Best served hot.

Red Eye Gravy. Use the juices left in the skillet as a base. Heat juices in skillet until they smoke. Add about three ounces of water for every three ham slices. A good Tennessee Country Ham will make red eye gravy without adding coffee. When liquid comes to a boil, remove to a serving bowl or pour over fried ham slices on a deep serving platter. Serve immediately!

COUNTRY HAM-STUFFED APPLES

⅓ cup raisins
1 tablespoon Jack Daniel's Whiskey
1 cup finely chopped country ham
3 tablespoons butter, softened
¼ cup chopped pecans
3 tablespoons brown sugar
2 tablespoons lemon juice
4 large baking apples (Winesaps are best), unpeeled and cored
¼ cup cider vinegar

Soak raisins in Jack Daniel's Whiskey, stirring often, for 30 minutes. Preheat oven to 350°. Combine ham, butter, raisins and whiskey, pecans

and brown sugar. Place apples in a greased baking dish; sprinkle lemon juice inside cavity. Divide filling evenly among apples. Bake for 40 to 45 minutes, basting outside of apples with vinegar. Makes 4 servings.

SINFULLY GOOD ROAST PORK

1 cup pitted prunes, halved
½ cup dried apricots, halved
½ to 1 cup Jack Daniel's Whiskey
1 teaspoon grated lemon rind
1 teaspoon grated orange rind
½ peeled apple, cut into ½-inch chunks
1 tablespoon honey
1 4 to 5-pound pork loin roast, boned and butterflied
Salt and pepper to taste
1 garlic clove
4 tablespoons sweet butter, softened
1 tablespoon dried thyme
2 tablespoons all-purpose flour
1 to 1½ cups apple cider

Place prunes and apricots in a bowl. Pour Jack Daniel's Whiskey over fruit; soak for 2 to 3 hours, until fruit has absorbed most of the whiskey. Add lemon and orange rinds, apple and honey; mix gently. Drain and reserve extra liquid. Preheat oven to 325°F. Open pork loin and sprinkle with salt and pepper. Place fruit in a strip a few inches from ends of loin. (Make sure fruit strip stops about 1½ inches from ends of meat to prevent fruit from falling out when meat is rolled.) Gently roll meat up around fruit. Tie securely with butcher's twine at 2-inch intervals. Cut garlic into slivers, and with a sharp knife punch deep slits in roast and insert garlic. Rub softened butter on outside of roast; sprinkle with thyme. Dust with flour. Place roast on rack in roasting pan. Pour cider and reserved liquid over meat; place pan in center of oven. Roast 25 minutes per pound, basting frequently; add cider or water if necessary. Remove roast from pan; set aside, covered loosely with foil, for 20 to 30 minutes before cutting. Spoon pan juices over each slice. Makes 6 to 8 servings.

Deep South Flamed Veal

6 thin slices of veal
2 cups soft white bread crumbs
2 tablespoons chopped parsley
1 clove garlic, crushed
  Freshly ground black pepper
¼ teaspoon marjoram
¼ teaspoon dried thyme
1 teaspoon salt
¼ cup butter, melted
2 tablespoons vegetable oil
1 cup chicken stock
⅓ cup Jack Daniel's Whiskey
  Hot cooked rice

Flatten veal steaks slightly between two sheets of waxed paper. Combine bread crumbs, parsley, garlic, pepper, marjoram, thyme, salt and melted butter. If desired, add 2 teaspoons of Jack Daniel's Whiskey to this mixture. Place about 2 tablespoons of the mixture on each slice of veal; roll up and secure with toothpicks. Coat lightly with flour. Heat oil in a large pan; quickly brown veal on both sides. Add chicken stock and Jack Daniel's Whiskey; lower heat and simmer 15 to 20 minutes or until meat is tender. Serve with rice. Veal may be flamed with an extra 2 teaspoons of Jack Daniel's Whiskey when served. Makes 6 servings.

Country-Style Steak and Gravy

4 4-ounce minute steaks (cubed round steak)
3 eggs, beaten
1 cup all-purpose flour
2 teaspoons pepper
1 cup lard or bacon drippings
1½ cups milk
  Salt to taste

Dip steaks in beaten eggs. Mix flour with half the pepper and roll steaks in mixture. Dip steaks in egg again and roll in flour. Heat lard or drippings in a heavy skillet. Fry steaks until brown on both sides. Remove from heat and drain. Pour off all but 2 tablespoons fat in skillet. Sprinkle in 2 tablespoons leftover flour and stir, scraping up browned bits of crust. Slowly add milk; cook until thickened. Season with salt and pepper. Serve over steaks. Makes 4 servings.

Boarding House Meat Loaf

Barbara Ruth McGowan is the cook at Miss Mary's who specializes in cooking meat entrées. It stands to reason that she is loved by everyone except vegetarians, of which there aren't too many in this neck of the woods. Her barbecued ribs, beef pot roast, country fried steak, and liver and onions start mouths watering at the mere thought of them. For this cookbook, Barbara Ruth shares her Boarding House Meat Loaf, a winner any time, any day!

1½ pounds ground beef
¾ cup uncooked oatmeal
1½ teaspoons salt
¼ cup chopped green pepper
¼ cup chopped onion
¼ cup catsup
2 eggs, beaten
  Meat Loaf Sauce

Preheat oven to 350°. Combine all the ingredients and form into loaf. Place into a greased 9x3-inch loaf pan. Bake for 1 hour. Pour off juice and bake about 10 minutes longer. Place on platter and cover with sauce. Makes 6 to 8 servings.

MEAT LOAF SAUCE

¾ cup catsup
2 tablespoons chopped onion
2 tablespoons chopped green pepper
¼ cup firmly packed brown sugar

Simmer over low heat until onion and pepper are tender.

Black Label Sirloin Roast

1 4-pound beef sirloin roast
2 cups catsup
¼ cup Jack Daniel's Whiskey
2 tablespoons Worcestershire sauce
½ cup dark brown sugar
¼ cup lemon juice

Preheat oven to 350°. Place roast on rack in shallow roasting pan. Combine all remaining ingredients in a saucepan; heat until sugar melts. Baste roast with sauce and cook 2 hours for rare (140° on meat thermometer) or 2½ hours for medium (160°). Baste frequently during cooking time. Makes 8 to 10 servings.

Tenderloin Tips

2 pounds beef tenderloin tips, thinly sliced
4 tablespoons butter
2 teaspoons salt
1 cup sliced mushrooms
¼ cup chopped onion
1 clove garlic, minced
½ cup Burgundy wine
½ cup Jack Daniel's Whiskey
1 cup crushed canned tomatoes
2 beef bouillon cubes
2 teaspoons sugar
  Mashed potatoes

Sauté meat quickly in butter, half at a time, until browned. Add salt, mushrooms, onion and garlic; simmer for several minutes, adding extra butter if needed. Add wine, Jack Daniel's Whiskey, tomatoes, bouillon cubes and sugar. Simmer for 30 minutes or until tender. Serve with mashed potatoes. Makes 4 servings.

FARMHOUSE COUNTRY FRIED STEAK

There is a saying in these parts that if you don't have a little politics to flavor your gravy in the morning you can hardly make it through the day. That may illustrate how important a visit from the governor is to country and city folk alike.

Some time back, former Tennessee governor Lamar Alexander came to Lynchburg for a ribbon-cutting ceremony to kick off his year-long state celebration of Homecoming '86. The Mr. Jack Daniel's Original Silver Cornet Band turned out to welcome him. They played such favorites as "Hail, Hail the Gang's All Here." "The Bear Went Over the Mountain," and "Hot Time in the Ol' Town Tonight." The whole town and half the county turned out. But the best part of the day was the dinner served at Miss Mary Bobo's Boarding House. It started with Lynchburg Lemonade on the lawn and finished with a delectable pie. My favorite dish was country fried steak and included gravy thickened with buttermilk, cheese—and the right amount of politics for flavor.

2 pounds round steak
½ teaspoon salt
½ teaspoon pepper
½ cup all-purpose flour
1 tablespoon vegetable oil
1 onion, chopped
1 cup chicken stock or water
1 cup buttermilk
1 cup shredded cheese

Divide steak into serving pieces. Pound with a kitchen mallet or rim of saucer until thin. Sprinkle with salt and pepper; dust with flour. In a skillet, heat oil and sear meat until evenly brown on all sides. Add onion and cook several minutes until limp. Combine chicken stock and buttermilk and pour over meat. Stir to loosen up crust from the bottom of the skillet. Cover and cook over medium-low heat until meat is tender, 45 to 50 minutes. Add cheese and stir into gravy. This is delicious over rice or biscuits. Makes 6 to 8 servings.

BEEF STEW

2 teaspoons all-purpose flour
2 teaspoons salt
1 teaspoon pepper
2 pounds stew beef, cut into 1-inch cubes
2 tablespoons vegetable oil
1 clove garlic, minced
½ cup Jack Daniel's Whiskey
2 cups water
2 10½-ounce cans beef broth
½ pound frozen small whole onions
½ pound whole baby carrots
2 medium potatoes, cubed
1 10-ounce package frozen lima beans

Mix flour, salt and pepper in a plastic bag. Place meat in bag; shake to coat meat well. In Dutch oven or heavy saucepan, brown meat in oil. Add garlic, Jack Daniel's Whiskey, water and broth. Bring to a boil. Lower heat; simmer for two hours or until meat is tender. Add onions, carrots, potatoes and lima beans. Cook until vegetables are tender. Makes 6 servings.

CITY PATÉ
Translation: Extra Fancy Country Meat Loaf

1¼ pounds ground veal
½ pound bulk sausage
3 pounds ground pork
¼ pound ground chicken
1 clove garlic, minced
½ cup finely chopped green onions with tops
4 tablespoons butter, divided
½ pound chicken livers
¼ cup Jack Daniel's Whiskey
¼ cup heavy cream
1 teaspoon vinegar
2 teaspoons all-purpose flour
1 egg, beaten
½ teaspoon nutmeg
2 teaspoons salt
½ teaspoon pepper
  Strips of blanched fat bacon
  French bread

Preheat oven to 350°. Combine ground meats in large mixing bowl. In a skillet, sauté garlic and green onion in 2 tablespoons butter until tender; add to meat mixture. Lightly sauté chicken livers in remaining butter; remove from skillet. Grind chicken livers and add to other ground meats. Pour Jack Daniels' Whiskey into previously used skillet; stir for several minutes. Add cream, vinegar, flour, egg, nutmeg, salt, pepper and Jack Daniel's Whiskey to meat mixture; blend well. Line loaf pan with slightly overlapping blanched bacon, allowing enough to hang over sides to fold over top of meat mixture. Place the meat mixture in pan; fold bacon strips over meat, covering completely. Cover and place the pan into a larger pan of boiling water. Bake for 2 hours or until juices run clear. Remove from oven; refrigerate until serving time. Slice very thin and serve with French bread. Makes 4 pounds of paté.

SUPREME BURGERS

2 pounds ground chuck
½ teaspoon salt
½ teaspoon pepper
¼ cup heavy cream
2 teaspoons vegetable oil
2 tablespoons shallots, minced
1½ cups sliced fresh mushrooms
¼ cup Jack Daniel's Whiskey
½ cup heavy cream
1 large tomato, chopped
2 tablespoons minced parsley
¼ teaspoon basil
1 teaspoon salt

Combine ground chuck, salt, pepper and ¼ cup cream. Shape into six patties. In large skillet, add oil and pan-broil over medium heat until desired degree of doneness. Remove to heated platter. Keep in warm oven while preparing sauce. Cook shallots and mushrooms in pan drippings until tender. Add remaining ingredients and cook for several minutes. Pour sauce over patties. Makes 6 servings.

SPAGHETTI AND BEEF CASSEROLE

Mary Ruth Hall is now a hostess at Miss Mary Bobo's Boarding House, but back in 1949 and 1950 she was a boarder there. As a Home Extension Agent with the State of Tennessee, she paid $12.50 per week for room and board. At the time she was the only lady boarder, so she stayed in bed each morning until the men finished shaving in the bathroom that they all shared. A delightful lady with a great sense of humor, here she shares her favorite casserole.

3 tablespoons butter
2 pounds ground beef
2 medium onions, chopped
2 4-ounce cans mushroom stems and pieces, undrained
2 8-ounce cans tomato sauce
1 6-ounce can tomato paste
1 teaspoon ground oregano
1 teaspoon garlic powder
2 7-ounce packages spaghetti
1 8-ounce package cream cheese, softened
2 cups cottage cheese
½ cup chopped fresh or frozen chives
½ cup sour cream
½ cup fine buttered bread crumbs

Possum and Sweet 'Taters

Some recipes are so rich—or maybe we should say so wild and gamey—that they just "needs be included." The following is just such a recipe from our good friend, Herb Fanning.

First, you must catch Br'er Possum without injuring him in any way. Many old timers just climbed the tree, grabbed him by the nape of the neck, and dropped him into a potato sack. However, Br'er Possum has a mighty bad habit of going out on a limb where the hunter can't follow. In this case, have someone hold the dog while the fellow up the tree gets hold of the limb as far out as possible and shakes Br'er Possum off the limb. The man on the ground grabs Br'er Possum and puts him into the sack while he is still confused by the fall.

With a good dog and a damp, still night, you should be able to have at least four or five possums in your sack by ten or eleven o'clock.

It is common knowledge that Br'er Possum is not too fastidious about his diet, and so you should have a crate at home where you can keep him and feed him table scraps for about a week before you dress him for cooking.

To properly prepare Br'er Possum for the oven, select a fat one from the crate. Grasp him by both hind legs, place a stick across his neck, step on the stick with both feet and pull until something gives—which will be his neck.

By all means, dress him by removing the hair only. Never skin him. For this purpose, you need a container that will hold about five gallons of hot water. If available, add a double handful of hardwood ashes to the water. The temperature of the water should be 155° F. When all the hair is removed, finish dressing in the usual manner, although you may leave the head on.

Soak Br'er Possum for 12 hours or more in cold water to which one cup of salt has been added, drain off, and rinse with boiling water. Stuff with your favorite dressing, put in the roaster with a little water, and cook at 350° F. for about an hour and a half. Baste every 15 minutes with pan drippings. After the possum has cooked for 1½ hours, add several medium-sized sweet potatoes. If you did not remove the possum's head, place one sweet potato in his mouth, à la roast pig.

Heat butter in a heavy skillet. Add ground beef and onion; sauté until meat is browned, stirring to crumble. Drain off pan drippings. Combine mushrooms, tomato sauce, tomato paste, oregano, and garlic powder. Add to meat mixture; mix well. Simmer, uncovered, for 15 minutes. Cook spaghetti according to package directions; drain. Place half of spaghetti in a buttered 9x13-inch baking dish. Combine cream cheese, cottage cheese, chives and sour cream; mix well. Spoon cream cheese mixture over spaghetti layer, spreading evenly. Place remaining spaghetti over cream cheese mixture. Pour meat sauce over spaghetti and sprinkle with buttered bread crumbs. Preheat oven to 350°. Bake for 30 minutes or until bubbly. Makes 12 servings.

MACARONI AND CHEESE PUFF

½ cup uncooked elbow macaroni
1½ cups milk, scalded
2 cups (½ pound) shredded sharp cheddar cheese, divided
1 cup soft bread crumbs
¼ cup diced pimiento
3 tablespoons melted butter
1 tablespoon chopped parsley
1 tablespoon grated onion
½ teaspoon salt
3 eggs, separated
¼ teaspoon cream of tartar

Cook macaroni according to package directions; drain and set aside. Combine milk and 1½ cups cheese, stirring until cheese melts. Add macaroni, bread crumbs, pimiento, butter, parsley, onion and salt. Beat egg yolks and stir into mixture. Preheat oven to 350°. Beat egg whites and cream of tartar until stiff but not dry; fold into macaroni mixture. Spoon into a lightly greased 2-quart baking dish. Bake about 50 minutes or until set. Sprinkle with remaining cheese. Return to oven and bake 5 minutes longer or until cheese melts. Makes 6 servings.

HEN FRUIT CASSEROLE

Butter and egg money generally has always been set aside for the lady of the house to spend on the little luxuries otherwise not allowed for in the budget. (A farmer's income is about as predictable as the weather). However, at times there were more eggs than could be sold or consumed in the usual day-to-day fare. A natural solution to this were recipes that would take advantage of the untimely abundance. Such is the following recipe and since fruit-bearing time is when you have an "abundance of fruit," the name seems to be appropriate.

2 dozen eggs
2 cups mayonnaise
2 cups sour cream
1 2-ounce bottle of capers, drained
1 tablespoon dill weed
 Salt and pepper to taste
1 teaspoon minced parsley
1 tablespoon finely chopped onion
 Day-old bread

Boil eggs; cool in cold water after cracking each egg gently (allows shells to slip off easily). Slice eggs in half lengthwise and place in a large greased casserole. Preheat oven to 300°. Mix remaining ingredients, except bread. Pour over eggs to cover. Bake for only 30 minutes. Do not overcook because sauce will curdle. Serve over toasted day-old bread slices. Makes 10 to 12 servings.

FANCY EGGS FOR THE IN-LAWS

4 medium tomatoes
 Salt and pepper
1 clove garlic, minced
4 large eggs
3 tablespoons tomato sauce
3 tablespoons heavy cream
½ teaspoon dried thyme
4 tablespoons grated Parmesan cheese
4 slices bread, cut into rounds
 Butter
 Parsley

Slice off the stem end of the tomatoes and scoop out the pulp being careful not to puncture the shell. Sprinkle insides with salt and pepper and turn upside down to drain for 30 minutes. Preheat oven to 350°. Sprinkle a little minced garlic inside each shell and arrange in a greased baking dish. Break an egg into each tomato. Combine tomato sauce, cream and thyme. Spoon evenly over the egg. Top with cheese. Bake for 30 minutes or until eggs are set. Butter and toast bread rounds. Arrange one tomato on each toast round and garnish with parsley. Makes 4 servings.

WEEPING LEG OF LAMB

1 4½ to 5-pound leg of lamb
3 cloves garlic, cut into slivers
  Salt and pepper to taste
1 teaspoon dried rosemary leaves
6 to 8 potatoes, peeled and thinly sliced
1 small onion, thinly sliced
¼ cup butter
1 cup beef bouillon
¼ cup Parmesan cheese

Preheat oven to 325°. With an ice pick or sharp knife, poke holes in the surface of the lamb and insert slivers of garlic. Rub with salt, pepper and rosemary. In a buttered baking dish, arrange potato slices overlapping; repeat with onion slices and dot with butter and salt and pepper. Repeat layers. Pour bouillon over all. Place lamb on potatoes. Roast for 1½ to 2 hours or until lamb reaches an internal temperature of 135° (for rare roast) and potatoes are browned and crusty. (If potatoes are done first, remove them and continue cooking the lamb.) Sprinkle potatoes with Parmesan cheese and leave in oven long enough to melt. Carve leg of lamb separately and lay slices over potatoes to serve. Makes 8 servings.

FRIED FISH PATTIES

2 cups stiff mashed potatoes
2 egg yolks, beaten
½ cup finely chopped onion
  Salt and pepper to taste
2 cups flaked cooked fish
½ cup cornmeal
¼ cup corn oil

Combine mashed potatoes, egg yolks, onion and seasonings. Add flaked fish and form mixture into small patties. Roll in cornmeal. Heat oil in skillet over medium heat. Add patties and fry until golden brown on both sides. Makes 4 servings.

ROLLED STUFFED FILETS OF SOLE

4 slices bacon
2 medium onions, finely chopped
1 clove garlic, minced
1½ cups finely chopped mushrooms
1 tomato, peeled, seeded and finely chopped
  Salt and pepper to taste
8 large (6-ounce each) filets of sole
½ cup dry white wine
8 thin lemon slices

Preheat oven to 350°. Cook bacon in a heavy skillet until crisp. Remove bacon from skillet. Chop when cooled. Set aside. Remove all but 2 tablespoons drippings from pan. Sauté onion, garlic and mushrooms until tender. Add tomato, salt and pepper; continue cooking for several minutes. Stir in chopped bacon. Spread fish with stuffing mixture and roll up, starting at the wide end. Fasten with toothpicks and arrange in a shallow greased baking dish. Pour in wine and bake for 20 minutes or until fish flakes easily with a fork but is not dry. Garnish each filet with a lemon slice. Makes 8 servings.

SOUTHERN FRIED CATFISH

4 to 6 catfish, skinned with heads cut off
  Salt and pepper to taste
½ cup white cornmeal
¼ cup all-purpose flour
1 egg, beaten
  Lard or vegetable oil

Salt and pepper fish. Mix cornmeal and flour together. Roll fish in cornmeal-flour mixture, then dip into beaten egg. Roll in cornmeal-flour mixture again; set aside. Heat lard or oil to 375° (very hot) in a heavy skillet. Add fish and lightly brown on both sides. Makes 4 to 6 servings.

Southern Food, Something Special

S ettlers that came to Tennessee came with the spirit of pioneers—open-minded and adventurous. It was with this spirit that men built homes and plantations, planted their crops and the women prepared their table fare.

The South represents a mixture and blending of people and cultures that settled here, and Southern food reflects this blend in the recipes and foods the settlers brought with them. Seeds and tubers, plants and cuttings were brought across the high mountains by wagon or down rivers by flatboat. Southern soil was rich with all kinds of berries and fruit, nuts and vegetables, which, added to these transported plants, provided an abundance of ingredients for creative cooks. From the Cherokee Indians, the pioneers learned to make hoe cakes, small cakes of cornmeal mush fried in iron skillets over a fire. Cattle and livestock flourished in lush pastures, providing meat and dairy products in good supply. Game and fish were plentiful and excellent additions to the table.

Slaves brought okra seeds and yam tubers with them from their native Africa. Both of these vegetables are staples in Southern cooking. Especially fond of well-seasoned foods, their creative preparation of the bountiful Southern harvest has given us an undeniable and inescapable legacy.

After the Civil War, the South recovered slowly. The diet that evolved was one of foods that were easy to come by—butter, cream and eggs, fresh vegetables, cornmeal for bread, chicken and ham.

Southern cuisine is as rich in heritage as it is in ingredients, but it is usually simple fare. We have eaten everything from turnip greens and cornbread in the lean years to country ham and oysters with important guests. Using the best from available resources and the freshest produce, our simple preparation renders the most delectable of dishes.

"Snapper Daniel"

This recipe was created by Chris Nelson and Sheila Hutchinson, Choices Bar and Grill, Chicago, Illinois.

    1 medium size shallot, minced
    4 tablespoons butter
    ¼ cup Jack Daniel's Whiskey
    2 cups heavy cream
    ½ cup sliced mushrooms
    4 6-ounce (each) red snapper filets

Sauté shallot in butter. Add Jack Daniel's Whiskey. Heat until liquor is burned off. Add cream slowly while stirring over low heat; add mushrooms and heat until softened. Broil snapper until it flakes easily with a fork. Serve sauce over fish. Makes 4 servings.

BBQ Fish Bake

    3 to 4 pounds fresh fish (filets or whole fish)
        Salt and pepper to taste
    ¼ cup chopped onion
    2 tablespoons vegetable oil
    2 tablespoons vinegar
    2 tablespoons brown sugar
    1 cup catsup
    3 tablespoons Worcestershire sauce
    1 teaspoon chopped parsley
    ¼ cup lemon juice

Preheat oven to 425°. Sprinkle fish with salt and pepper and place in greased pan. Sauté onion in oil until tender. Add remaining ingredients. Cook over low heat for 5 minutes. Pour over fish. Bake for 30 to 40 minutes or until fish flakes easily with a fork. Makes 6 servings.

Pasta with Inebriated Clam Sauce

    2 tablespoons vegetable oil
    2 tablespoons minced shallots
    1½ cups clams, drained
    ¼ cup Jack Daniel's Whiskey
    1½ cups tomatoes, peeled, seeded and chopped
    ½ teaspoon dried oregano
    ½ teaspoon dried basil
    ½ cup heavy cream
        Salt and pepper
    1 pound pasta (fettucine, linguine, or spaghetti),
        cooked al dente

Heat oil in heavy skillet. Add shallots and sauté for 30 seconds. Add clams and stir until heated through. Pour in Jack Daniel's Whiskey and carefully ignite. Allow flame to burn out. Stir in tomatoes, oregano and basil. Bring sauce to a boil. Remove from heat; stir in cream. Salt and pepper to taste. Serve over hot pasta. Makes 4 servings.

Moore County Oysters

    2 tablespoons butter
    1½ tablespoons all-purpose flour
    1 cup milk or half-and-half
        Salt and pepper
    2½ cups cracker crumbs
    1 pint shucked oysters with juice
    ¼ cup butter

Melt butter over low heat. Stir in flour. Slowly add milk; stir until thickened. Season with salt and pepper. Preheat oven to 350°. Grease 1½-quart casserole. Layer 1 cup cracker crumbs on bottom of dish. Cover with half the oysters, then half the sauce. Repeat layers of crumbs, oysters and sauce, reserving some for top layer. Sprinkle with reserved crumbs. Dot with butter. Bake for 15 to 20 minutes or until brown and bubbly. Makes 4 to 6 servings.

Shrimp and Artichoke Casserole

6½ tablespoons butter, divided
4½ tablespoons all-purpose flour
¾ cup milk
¾ cup heavy cream
    Salt and pepper to taste
1 20-ounce can artichoke hearts (not marinated) or 1
    10-ounce package frozen artichoke hearts, cooked
    as directed on package
1 pound shrimp, cooked, shelled and deveined
1 pound mushrooms, sliced
¼ cup dry sherry
1 tablespoon Worcestershire sauce
¼ cup Parmesan cheese, grated
    Paprika

Preheat oven to 375°. Melt 4½ tablespoons butter in saucepan and stir in flour. Slowly whisk in milk and cream. Stir until mixture is thickened. Season with salt and pepper. Arrange the artichokes on the bottom of a greased baking dish. Layer shrimp over artichokes. Cook the mushrooms in the remaining butter until tender. Spoon mushrooms over shrimp and artichokes. Add the sherry and Worcestershire sauce to the cream sauce and pour over shrimp mixture. Sprinkle with Parmesan cheese and paprika. Bake for 20 to 25 minutes or until bubbly. Makes 6 servings.

JUBILEE SHRIMP

1½ cups heavy cream
4 tablespoons unsalted butter, clarified
12 large shrimp, peeled, deveined and butterflied (tails intact)
4 medium shallots, minced
6 tablespoons Jack Daniel's Whiskey
Salt and freshly ground white pepper to taste
Minced fresh parsley

Simmer cream in heavy saucepan over medium heat until reduced by half. Heat butter in large heavy skillet over medium-high heat. Add shrimp, cut-side down; cook until just opaque, about 1 minute on each side. Remove shrimp from skillet. Stir in shallots and sauté until soft, about 2 minutes (do not brown). Drain off butter. Remove pan from heat. Pour Jack Daniel's Whiskey into corner of skillet, heat and carefully ignite, shaking pan gently until flames subside. Add reduced cream; simmer until reduced by ⅓. Season with salt and pepper. Return shrimp to skillet and heat thoroughly. Divide among heated plates. Sprinkle with parsley. Serve immediately. Makes 2 servings.

SHRIMP FLAMBÉ

¼ cup butter
3 tablespoons vegetable oil
1 clove garlic, minced
1 small onion, grated
¾ pound deveined raw shrimp
Salt and pepper to taste
3 tablespoons finely minced parsley
Juice of 1 lemon
2 to 3 tablespoons Jack Daniel's Whiskey

Melt butter and oil in skillet. Add garlic and onion. Cook several minutes until tender but not brown. Add shrimp, salt and pepper. Cover; simmer several minutes, turning shrimp once. Add parsley and lemon juice. Turn off heat and add Jack Daniel's Whiskey. Carefully ignite, allow flame to burn out; serve. Makes 2 to 4 servings.

OUTDOOR COOKING

ZUCCHINI AND TOMATO SALAD

4 small zucchini
4 tomatoes
6 green onions
Lettuce leaves
3 tablespoons vinegar
1 teaspoon Dijon-style mustard
½ cup vegetable oil
Salt and pepper to taste

Cut zucchini into julienne strips; steam until just tender. Chill. Cut tomatoes into narrow wedges. Thinly slice green onions including some of the green tops. Combine vinegar and mustard. Slowly whisk in oil. Season with salt and pepper. Arrange lettuce leaves on serving plates. Layer tomatoes and zucchini. Spoon dressing over vegetables. Top with onion. This is delicious with grilled meats. Makes 6 to 8 servings.

BROILED TOMATOES WITH DILL DRESSING

1 cup sour cream
½ cup mayonnaise
¼ cup finely chopped green onion
2 teaspoons minced fresh dill
½ teaspoon salt
8 large ripe tomatoes
Salt
Pepper
8 teaspoons butter

Combine sour cream, mayonnaise, green onion, dill and salt. Set aside. Remove stems from tomatoes; cut in half crosswise. Sprinkle cut sides with salt and pepper to taste. Dot with butter. Broil 3 to 5 inches from heat for 5 minutes. Serve warm with dill dressing. This is an excellent side dish with grilled fish. Makes 8 to 10 servings.

Pool Room Slaw

1 medium head cabbage, grated or finely chopped
1 medium onion, grated
¼ cup sugar
3 teaspoons mustard
½ teaspoon salt
½ teaspoon celery seed
  Sweet pickle juice to taste
  Sweet pickles

Combine cabbage and onion. Blend the sugar, mustard, salt, celery seed and pickle juice. Pour dressing over the cabbage mixture; toss until well coated. Chill before serving. Garnish with pickle slices. This is delicious on grilled hamburgers. Makes 6 to 8 servings.

Note: This is the famous slaw served on the hamburgers at the Pool Room on the square in Fayetteville. Ladies never went inside *except* to pick up a take-out order of Pool Room Hamburgers. (Even the men wouldn't deny that!)

Bacon Grilled Corn

6 ears corn
6 strips uncooked bacon

To grill, pull down the husks but do not remove. Pull off silks. Replace the husks. Soak ears of corn in cold water for one hour. Pull down husks and wrap a strip of bacon spiral-fashion around ear. Replace husks. Tie husks together with piece of wet string or strip of husk. Arrange ears on the grill. Turn often for approximately 30 minutes. Discard bacon before serving. Makes 6 servings.

Corn Light Bread

2 cups cornmeal
1 cup all-purpose flour
½ cup sugar
1 teaspoon baking soda
1 teaspoon salt
3 tablespoons bacon drippings
2 cups buttermilk

Preheat oven to 300°. Combine cornmeal, flour, sugar, soda and salt. Add bacon drippings and buttermilk, beating well. Pour into a greased and floured 9x5x3-inch loaf pan (pan with a dark, dull finish will produce a crispier crust). Bake for 1 hour and 15 minutes or until brown. Remove from pan immediately. Corn light bread slices are delicious with barbecued meats. Makes 1 loaf.

Grilled Lemon Chicken

⅓ cup butter
¼ cup lemon juice
3 tablespoons water
1 tablespoon soy sauce
½ teaspoon paprika
1 teaspoon honey
½ teaspoon Dijon-style mustard
1 clove garlic, minced
¼ teaspoon salt
  Dash of cayenne pepper
1 2 to 2½-pound frying chicken, quartered

In a small saucepan, combine butter, lemon juice, water, soy sauce, paprika, honey, mustard, garlic, salt and cayenne pepper. Heat until butter melts, stirring well. Place chicken quarters over medium coals and grill about 15 minutes per side or until chicken juices run clear when pierced with a fork. Brush frequently with sauce. Makes 4 servings.

Pit Barbecue

. . . .

Folks everywhere will agree that pit barbecue is just about the best eating there is. At this point the disagreements begin. That is, everyone has his own ideas on how to prepare barbecue. Tennesseans are right in line with the rest of the world when it comes to how to barbecue, what to barbecue, and saucing the barbecue—they have a mind of their own. For those who have never done it and want to give it a try, here is how we do it.

To begin. Somewhere out back, in the yard or behind the garage, dig a pit, 4 feet long by 4 feet wide by 4 feet deep. Go to a metal workshop and have a piece of corrugated iron cut 4½' x4½', big enough to cover the top of the pit. If you can, also get a large iron oven box with a lid to use in the pit. This will eliminate having to lower more than one iron roaster down onto the coals and you can put meat, beans, corn, onions—the whole blamed dinner—into the container. However, if you can't get an oven box, then have an abundance of heavy iron pots and roasters with lids—one for each dish you cook. (Now some people do not use pots, but add three to four shovelfuls of sand on the coals and place the burlap-covered meat onto the sand. We use roasters; the choice is yours.)

Twenty hours before serving. On the day before you plan your party, fill the pit with wood and then stack more wood up three feet higher than ground level. Ignite, and let the wood burn down to coals in the pit. While the fire is burning, the meal should be assembled on a truck bed, table, or workspace nearby.

What to barbecue. Beef briskets, chuck roasts, rump roasts, spareribs, short ribs, fresh hams, pork shoulders, sausage, chicken—in fact, barbecue anything that suits your fancy. Do some of each!

The sauce
1 gallon catsup
1 pint cider vinegar
2 pounds brown sugar
6 tablespoons dry mustard
6 onions, finely chopped
6 cloves of garlic, minced
2 bottles of Worcestershire sauce
6 tablespoons of chili powder
1 cup of Jack Daniel's Whiskey

Mix all ingredients together. *Note:* If this is made a week or two before and refrigerated, the flavors will meld and ripen to a full body. If you do this, stir every day or so to keep the flavors working together.

With your hands, coat each piece of meat with the sauce, then wrap in cheesecloth or muslin. Then wrap in wet burlap. Place the meat in the one large iron roaster or in individual kettles. When all the meat is ready and the wood has burned down to coals in the bottom of the pit, lower the assembled roasters into the pit on top of the coals.

Vegetables. To roast ears of corn, carefully pull back the husk from the ear without removing it. Remove silks, brush the ear with butter, and pull the husk back over the ear of corn. Place in a wet burlap bag with potatoes, onions, or whatever. To cook dried beans, wash and pick over dried beans. Place beans in a large covered iron kettle. Fill with water, add salt, pepper, and salt pork to flavor. Cover and lower kettle into pit. If you are using the large iron roaster, place the kettle into the roaster and lower into the pit together.

Place the corrugated iron sheet over the top of the pit. Pile dirt around and over the edges to seal off any air supply to the pit. Leave the pit and do not remove the cover for eighteen hours.

Allow about a pound and a half of meat for each guest. Serve your dinner with ranch-cut bread, cole slaw, pickles, onion slices and for dessert, watermelon, of course.

The meal described is sure-fire pit ecstasy!

Tennessee Whiskey Chicken

This dish was created and served to The U.S. Conference of Mayors in June of 1987 when a call came from the Nashville Mayor's office to help give the conference a taste of Tennessee. It was created by Executive Chef Robert Siegel, Maude's Courtyard, Nashville, Tennessee.

2 small 2-pound frying chickens
1 cup Jack Daniel's Whiskey
  Salt and pepper
  Jack Daniel's Barrel chips

Have the butcher split 2 small fryers or if you prefer, buy cut-up chicken pieces. Place chicken in a shallow pan and douse with Jack Daniel's Whiskey. Sprinkle salt and pepper over the pieces; marinate for 2 hours. Soak some Jack Daniel's Barrel chips in water as you build a charcoal fire in your barbecue grill. Use the barrel chips in your grill to create a good smoking fire. Broil the fryers over the pit until well cooked. Serve with Whiskey Sauce. Makes 4 servings.

WHISKEY SAUCE

1 pound white mushrooms, sliced
6 green onions, chopped
2 tablespoons butter
2 ounces Jack Daniel's Whiskey
2 cups brown sauce*

Sauté the mushrooms and green onion in butter until tender. Add Jack Daniel's Whiskey and brown sauce and simmer until flavors have blended and the alcohol has evaporated. Keep warm until ready to serve.

*Note: To make brown sauce: Thicken beef bouillon with cornstarch or roux. Or better yet, make it from scratch.

Grilled Breast of Chicken With Maple Whiskey Glaze

1 teaspoon dried thyme
2 chicken breasts, boned, skinned and split
½ cup pure maple syrup
3 tablespoons Jack Daniel's Whiskey
1 tablespoon vegetable oil

Rub thyme over both sides of chicken breasts. Combine syrup, whiskey and oil. Marinate breasts in the refrigerator for several hours. Grill or broil breasts. Baste frequently with the marinade for a shiny brown glaze. (Glaze burns easily, so watch carefully.) Makes 2 servings.

GRILLED COUNTRY HAM

6 ¼-inch thick slices center-cut country ham
1 cup orange juice
¼ cup firmly packed light brown sugar
3 tablespoons vegetable oil

Cut slashes in fat to prevent ham from curling. Combine juice, sugar and oil. Pour over ham slices in a shallow pan. Marinate 1 hour before cooking. Grill ham over low heat 2 to 3 minutes per side. Baste with marinade during cooking. Be careful not to overcook. This is great with cheese grits. Makes 6 servings.

GRILLED CHUCK ROAST

⅓ cup Jack Daniel's Whiskey
⅓ cup brown sugar
⅓ cup soy sauce
⅓ cup water
1 tablespoon Worcestershire sauce
1 teaspoon lemon juice
⅛ teaspoon garlic powder
1 2 to 3-pound chuck roast
Jack Daniel's Barrel chips, soaked in water

Combine Jack Daniel's Whiskey, brown sugar, soy sauce, water, Worcestershire sauce, lemon juice and garlic powder; mix well. Place roast in plastic bag; add marinade and seal. Place in a dish; refrigerate overnight. Turn roast occasionally. Grill over medium coals with Jack Daniel's Barrel chips about 20 to 25 minutes per side for medium. Baste occasionally with marinade. To serve, cut into thin slices. Makes 4 to 6 servings.

OLD NO. 7 FLANK STEAK

1½ pounds ½-inch-thick flank steak
1 clove garlic, minced
2 teaspoons dry mustard

¼ cup Jack Daniel's Whiskey
Vegetable oil
2 tablespoons butter
Salt and freshly ground pepper

Score the flank steak, with a sharp knife, about ⅛-inch deep, in a diamond pattern. Mash the garlic with the mustard. Stir in the Jack Daniel's Whiskey. Pour mixture over the steak and refrigerate, covered, overnight. (Easiest done in a zip-lock bag.) Set out at room temperature for 2 hours before cooking. Grill, using charcoal or gas grill. Cook over high heat 3 to 5 minutes per side, dotting each side with butter while cooking. Slice the steak immediately by cutting across the grain into ¼-inch thick slices. Sprinkle with salt and pepper. Makes 4 servings.

OUTSIDE BURGERS

1½ pounds ground beef
½ cup uncooked quick-cooking oats
¼ cup finely chopped onion
1½ teaspoons salt
½ teaspoon pepper
⅔ cup tomato juice
½ teaspoon Worcestershire sauce

Combine all ingredients. Shape into 6 patties. Grill over coals to desired degree of doneness. Serve on buns with lettuce and tomato slices. Makes 6 servings.

BBQ LAMB CHOPS

8 1½-inch-thick rib lamb chops
4 cloves garlic, halved
Salt and pepper to taste
⅛ teaspoon powdered thyme
½ cup red wine vinegar
¼ cup vegetable oil

Rub chops with cut side of garlic; sprinkle with salt and pepper. Combine thyme, vinegar and oil; coat chops while preparing fire. Place grill 5 to 6 inches over medium heat. Grill lamb: 6 to 7 minutes per side for rare, 9 to 10 minutes per side for medium, 12 to 14 minutes per side for well done. Brush lamb often with vinegar mixture during cooking. Makes 8 servings.

SPECIAL GRILLED LAMB CHOPS

4 1-inch-thick lamb chops
½ cup Almost Homemade Mint Jelly
Vegetable oil
Salt and pepper

Prepare charcoal or gas grill for cooking. Trim all but ¼-inch fat from edges of lamb chops. Slash remaining fat at 1-inch intervals. Spread mint jelly over each side of the chop and set aside, covered, for one hour. Brush the grill with oil to prevent sticking. Sear chops over hot coals for 1 minute per side, including edges. Grill over medium-hot heat 4 minutes per side for rare, 5 minutes for medium-rare. Sprinkle with salt and pepper before serving. Makes 2 to 4 servings.

ALMOST HOMEMADE MINT JELLY

1 12-ounce jar apple-mint jelly
¼ cup green crème de menthe
1 tablespoon vinegar
½ cup chopped fresh mint leaves

In a large bowl, use a large wire whisk to combine all ingredients except mint until mixture is smooth. Add mint leaves. Chill overnight before serving. Makes 1½ cups.

SIMPLE GRILLED FISH STEAKS

4 fish steaks (swordfish, tuna, halibut or turbot)
1 cup Jack Daniel's Whiskey
Vegetable oil
Salt and pepper to taste

Marinate fish steaks in Jack Daniel's Whiskey in a zip-lock bag or shallow glass dish. Cover and set aside for 1 hour. Remove the fish steaks from the marinade and pat dry. Brush lightly with oil. Grill over hot coals, basting once with oil. Cook 5 minutes per side. Season with salt and pepper before serving. Makes 4 servings.

CAMP FIRE TROUT

4 *medium trout*
4 *to 8 slices bacon*
  Lemon wedges

Dry fish with paper towels. Wrap 1 or 2 slices of bacon around each trout and secure with toothpicks. Over moderately hot coals, cook fish 5 minutes per side or until flesh is white and bacon is done (be careful not to overcook). When done, fish will feel firm when prodded gently with finger and will flake easily with a fork. Garnish with lemon wedges. Makes 4 servings.

DOUBLE SHOT PORK OR POULTRY GLAZE

½ *cup Jack Daniel's Whiskey*
1⅓ *cups honey*
  3 *tablespoons lemon juice*
½ *teaspoon fresh ground black pepper*

Combine all ingredients. Serve as a sauce or glaze for grilled chicken or pork. Makes 2 cups.

Southern Hospitality

I f you were to ask any person who has visited the South to define his visit in two words, he would, in all probability, say "Southern hospitality." The South has long excelled in gracious entertaining so much so that it is considered indigenous to the region.

Long after the northeastern part of the United States became industrialized and citified, the South was still mostly rural communities, small farming and agricultural towns with a lot of country folk in between. Socializing was a highly prized affair, not just because of the distance involved between neighbors, but also because people earned their living off of the land, which left little time for leisure.

Social gatherings such as barn raisings, quilting bees, hog killings, cattle branding or crop harvesting were usually organized to help a neighbor. Whether working, visiting, or eating, helping each other was the core of hospitality. A kindly gathering of friends, family and strangers, sharing food and table and conversation of genuine interest to each other was entertainment that would be recalled when they returned to their remote farms.

It is this sincere caring for others, the thoughtful preparation of food generously provided, a nurturing of their community that has given Southerners a reputation of being a warm and hospitable people. The heart of the South shines in the act of hospitality.

Tennesseans have been hosts to the world by extending an invitation of *Y'all come to see us!* And come to see us they have. The warm sunny climate makes travel easy. The beauty and fragrance of honeysuckle and wild roses, magnolia trees and lilac bushes, along with the dazzling color of dogwood and azaleas, give pleasure to our senses. But visitors repeat again and again that the real enjoyment that they found was friendship extended, a sincere interest in conversation and a generous bounty of food shared in congenial atmosphere.

JACK DANIEL'S GRILLING SAUCE

½ cup pineapple juice
3 tablespoons soy sauce
1½ teaspoons ginger
½ teaspoon garlic powder
¼ cup Jack Daniel's Whiskey

Combine all ingredients and mix well. Dip meat in sauce and place on grill over hot coals. When meat is turned, brush with sauce. Grill to desired degree of doneness. Just before meat is removed from grill, brush again with sauce. Makes enough for 8 servings.

JACK DANIEL'S RIB GLAZE

1 cup Jack Daniel's Whiskey
½ cup dark brown sugar
1 cup catsup
2 teaspoons Worcestershire sauce
¼ cup vinegar
1 tablespoon fresh lemon juice
3 cloves garlic, minced
½ teaspoon dry mustard
Salt and pepper to taste

Combine all ingredients; mix well. Brush ribs with a thin coating of glaze and place on grill. Continue to baste when turning ribs. Makes enough for 2 racks of 7 to 10 ribs each.

JACK DANIEL'S MARINADE

¼ cup Jack Daniel's Whiskey
¼ cup soy sauce
¼ cup Dijon-style mustard
¼ cup minced green onions and tops
¼ cup firmly packed light brown sugar
1 teaspoon salt
Dash of Worcestershire sauce
Pepper to taste

Combine all ingredients. Blend well. Use to marinate shrimp or scallops for 1 hour or beef, chicken, or pork in the refrigerator overnight. Use to baste the shellfish or meat as it is grilled or broiled. Makes about 1¼ cups.

SPICED WHISKEY SAUCE FOR PORK

¼ cup Jack Daniel's Whiskey
¼ cup Dijon-style mustard
½ cup honey
¼ cup soy sauce
2 cloves garlic, minced
1 teaspoon Worcestershire sauce
¼ teaspoon powdered ginger
¼ cup corn oil

Combine all ingredients. Marinate pork in refrigerator overnight. Grill or broil, basting often with marinade. Makes 1½ cups.

SPECTACULAR SAUCE

½ clove garlic
2 tablespoons butter
2 tablespoons all-purpose flour
1 cup beef broth
1 tablespoon chopped fresh parsley or ½ teaspoon dried parsley

2 cups sliced fresh mushrooms
2 green onions, chopped
1 tablespoon butter
¼ cup Jack Daniel's Whiskey

Rub saucepan with garlic; discard garlic. Melt 2 tablespoons butter; stir in flour. Slowly add broth, stirring constantly. Add parsley; cook until thickened. Set aside. Sauté mushrooms and onion in butter until tender. Add Jack Daniel's Whiskey and thickened broth. Simmer several minutes over low heat. Serve over grilled or broiled chicken. Makes 2½ cups.

COOKOUT RELISH

2 cups finely chopped sweet pickles
2 tablespoons finely chopped green pepper
2 tablespoons finely chopped onion
1 tablespoon finely chopped pimiento
¼ teaspoon dry mustard
¼ teaspoon garlic powder
¼ cup Jack Daniel's Whiskey

Mix all ingredients and chill. Serve as a relish on hot dogs, grilled sausage or hamburgers. Makes 2½ cups.

PEPPER AND ONION RELISH SUPREME

5 green bell peppers
5 red bell peppers
5 onions, preferably Vidalia
1 cup apple cider vinegar
1 cup sugar
1 tablespoon salt
1 tablespoon mustard seed
1 tablespoon celery seed

Core peppers and cut into strips; place in a large stainless steel stew pan. Peel and slice onions; add to peppers. Combine vinegar, sugar and salt; stir to dissolve sugar. Add mustard seed and celery seed; pour vinegar mixture over all. Bring to a boil, then lower heat and simmer for 20 minutes, stirring occasionally. Skim off any foam and pour into clean, hot sterilized pint jars. Cool; cover with lid. Relish is ready for your backyard cookout. Spoon over hot dogs, hamburgers or eat as accompaniment for roast beef or pork. Makes 4 pints.

PICKLED EGGS

12 hard-boiled eggs
1 cup vinegar
2 tablespoons sugar
2 bay leaves
1 clove garlic, sliced
½ teaspoon celery seed
½ teaspoon mustard seed
1 cup water
1 teaspoon salt

At least two days before serving, boil eggs, cool and peel. Combine vinegar, sugar, bay leaves, garlic, celery seed, mustard seed, 1 cup water and 1 teaspoon salt; bring to a boil. Simmer covered for about 30 minutes. Cool. Place eggs in glass jar or pickle crock. Pour vinegar over eggs; cover and refrigerate 2 or 3 days. These are great for cookouts. Makes 12 pickled eggs.

DESSERTS

SNOCKERDOODLES

2 eggs, well beaten
½ cup vegetable oil
1 box devil's food cake mix
5 tablespoons Jack Daniel's Whiskey
Confectioners' sugar

Preheat oven to 350°. Blend eggs and oil. Add cake mix and Jack Daniel's Whiskey. Mix well. Form into small balls and roll in confectioners' sugar *before* baking. Place cookie balls on ungreased cookie sheet. Bake for 10 to 15 minutes at 350°. Be careful not to overbake . . . the cookies will be soft when taken from the oven. Makes 5 dozen.

CROWNING GLORY SAUCE

1 cup sugar
½ cup butter
½ cup half-and-half
¼ teaspoon cinnamon
Dash of nutmeg
¼ cup Jack Daniel's Whiskey

Melt sugar over medium heat in heavy skillet until light brown in color. Remove from heat and cool slightly. Add butter and stir until combined. Stir in remaining ingredients and cook until thickened. This is delicious as a sauce over ice cream, pound cake or bread pudding. Makes 1½ cups.

CHOCOLATE FONDUE

1 pound semi-sweet chocolate
½ cup heavy cream
¼ cup Jack Daniel's Whiskey

Melt chocolate; add cream and whiskey. Stir until smooth. Use as a dip for: graham crackers, bananas, strawberries, coffee cake, macaroons or oranges.

ROLLING PIN COOKIES

1 cup butter, softened
1 cup sugar
1 egg yolk
1 tablespoon grated semi-sweet chocolate
1 teaspoon salt
¼ teaspoon cinnamon
2 tablespoons Jack Daniel's Whiskey
2½ cups all-purpose flour
½ teaspoon baking powder
Chopped nuts

Cream butter and sugar until light and fluffy; beat in egg yolk, chocolate, salt and cinnamon. Add Jack Daniel's Whiskey, flour and baking powder; mix until dough holds together. Cover and refrigerate a few hours. Preheat oven to 350°. Use a floured rolling pin and lightly flour surface. Roll dough out very thin and cut with cookie cutter. Place cookies on ungreased cookie sheet; sprinkle with nuts. Bake for 10 minutes. Makes 6 dozen.

Note: Confectioners' sugar can be used (instead of flour) to roll dough out. It will give a slight glaze and eliminate any "flour" taste.

TENNESSEE CURLED COOKIES

1¼ cups sifted cake flour
⅔ cup sugar
1 teaspoon cinnamon
1 teaspoon ginger
¼ teaspoon salt
½ cup molasses
½ cup butter
3 tablespoons Jack Daniel's Whiskey
Sweetened whipped cream

Preheat oven to 300°. Sift dry ingredients together. Heat molasses until boiling; remove from heat, stir in butter until melted. Gradually stir in dry ingredients, then Jack Daniel's Whiskey. Drop by half-teaspoonful, 3 inches apart on greased cookie sheets, no more than 6 to a sheet. Bake for about 10 minutes. Cool 1 minute. Remove with a spatula and immediately roll around the handle of a wooden spoon. If cookies become too hard to remove or roll, return to oven for 30 seconds. Repeat with remaining batter. Store in an airtight container. These may be filled with whipped cream for a special treat. Makes about 5 dozen.

MINCEMEAT COOKIES

3¼ cups sifted all-purpose flour
½ teaspoon salt
1 teaspoon baking soda
1½ cups sugar
1 cup butter
3 eggs, beaten well
1½ cups mincemeat
2 tablespoons Jack Daniel's Whiskey

Preheat oven to 400°. Sift together flour, salt and soda. Combine sugar and butter and beat until fluffy. Add eggs, one at a time, beating well after each addition. Stir mincemeat and Jack Daniel's Whiskey into egg mixture. Gradually add flour mixture until combined. Drop by teaspoonful on greased baking sheet. Bake for 12 to 15 minutes. Makes 6 dozen.

TIPSY SPICE COOKIES

¼ cup Jack Daniel's Whiskey
1 8-ounce package dates, chopped
1 cup raisins
2 sticks butter, softened

1½ cups sugar
3 eggs
3 cups all-purpose flour
1 teaspoon baking soda
1½ teaspoons cinnamon
¼ teaspoon salt
½ teaspoon nutmeg
½ teaspoon cloves
1 cup chopped pecans

Pour Jack Daniel's Whiskey over dates and raisins; set aside for 1 hour or longer. Preheat oven to 350°. Blend butter and sugar with mixer until light and fluffy. Add eggs, one at a time, beating well after each addition. Combine the remaining ingredients. Stir into sugar mixture. Fold in fruit mixture. Drop by the teaspoonful onto greased cookie sheets. Bake for 12 to 15 minutes or until lightly browned. Makes 6 dozen.

TOFFEE SQUARES

1 cup sugar
1 cup butter, softened
¼ teaspoon salt
1 egg, separated
1 tablespoon Jack Daniel's Whiskey
2 teaspoons grated orange peel
2 cups sifted all-purpose flour
½ cup slivered almonds

Preheat oven to 300°. Beat sugar, butter and salt until creamy; add egg yolk, Jack Daniel's Whiskey and orange peel. Beat until smooth. Gradually stir in flour. Pat dough into a 9x13-inch pan. Beat egg white until foamy; spread over dough. Sprinkle with nuts. Bake for 40 to 45 minutes or until firm and lightly browned. Cut into squares while still warm. Makes about 3 dozen.

JACK DANIEL'S BROWNIES AND GLAZE

This recipe was prepared by Camelback and Central, 1403 2nd Avenue, New York, New York.

¾ cup all-purpose flour
½ teaspoon baking powder
½ teaspoon salt
6 tablespoons sweet butter
3 ounces baking chocolate
¾ cup sugar
2 eggs
1 cup chopped pecans or walnuts
1 teaspoon vanilla
2 ounces Jack Daniel's Whiskey
    Jack Daniel's Glaze

Mix together flour, baking powder and salt; set aside. Melt butter and chocolate in top of double boiler over simmering water. Remove from heat; add sugar, eggs, nuts, vanilla, flour mixture and Jack Daniel's Whiskey; mix well. Preheat oven to 350°. Pour batter into a greased 8x10-inch cake pan. Bake for approximately 25 minutes or until firm. Remove from oven; top with Glaze.

JACK DANIEL'S GLAZE

1 cup confectioners' sugar
1½ teaspoons boiling water
1½ tablespoons Jack Daniel's Whiskey
⅛ teaspoon vanilla

Combine all ingredients; stir till smooth. Brush on or pour over brownines.

ALMOND FUDGE BROWNIES

4 ounces unsweetened chocolate
⅔ cup butter
2 cups sugar
4 eggs, beaten

1 teaspoon almond extract
1¼ cups all-purpose flour
1 teaspoon baking powder
1 teaspoon salt
1 cup sliced almonds, toasted lightly
¼ cup Jack Daniel's Whiskey
2 cups confectioners' sugar
3 tablespoons butter, softened
3 tablespoons boiling water
1 teaspoon almond extract

Preheat oven to 350°. Melt chocolate and butter in large saucepan over low heat. Remove from heat. Mix in 2 cups sugar, eggs and almond extract. Sift together flour, baking powder and salt; stir into chocolate mixture. Stir in almonds and Jack Daniel's Whiskey. Spread in greased 9x13-inch pan; bake for 25 to 30 minutes or until a tester inserted in center comes out clean. Do not overbake. Place on rack to cool. To make glaze, pour confectioners' sugar into mixing bowl; add butter and begin to mix. Add boiling water and almond extract; beat until smooth. Frost cooled brownies. Makes 3 dozen.

GRANDMOTHER'S SHORTBREAD COOKIES

1 cup unsifted all-purpose flour
½ cup cornstarch
½ cup confectioners' sugar
¾ cup butter, softened
1 teaspoon almond extract

Sift flour, cornstarch and sugar together. Cream butter with dry ingredients; add almond extract. Refrigerate 1 hour. Preheat oven to 375°. Roll dough into small balls. Place on ungreased cookie sheet; flatten with fork. Bake for 10 to 12 minutes or until edges are lightly browned. Makes 3 dozen.

HOLIDATE BARS

1 8-ounce package pitted dates
1 cup pecans
1 cup confectioners' sugar
2 eggs, beaten
½ teaspoon salt
1 tablespoon vegetable oil
1 tablespoon lemon juice
¾ teaspoon nutmeg
Confectioners' sugar

Chop dates and pecans. Add sugar, eggs and salt. Add remaining ingredients; mix well. Spread in a lightly greased 9-inch square pan. Bake at 350° for 20 minutes. Cool slightly; cut into bars and roll gently in confectioners' sugar. Makes 20 bars.

TANYARD HILL WALNUT SQUARES

6 tablespoons all-purpose flour
½ teaspoon baking powder
4 tablespoons butter, softened
¾ cup firmly packed light brown sugar
1 egg, slightly beaten
4 tablespoons Jack Daniel's Whiskey, divided
½ teaspoon vanilla
1 cup walnuts, very finely chopped or ground
½ cup confectioners' sugar

Preheat oven to 350°. Combine flour and baking powder on piece of waxed paper. Grease and flour a 9x9x2-inch square baking pan. Beat butter and sugar in large bowl with electric mixer until light and fluffy, about 3 minutes. Beat in egg. Add 2 tablespoons Jack Daniel's Whiskey and vanilla. Stir in flour mixture and nuts just until blended. Spoon into pan. Bake for 15 to 20 minutes or until tester inserted in center comes out clean. Cool completely. Cut into 1-inch squares. Store in tin between layers of wax paper. To serve, drizzle each square with glaze made by combining confectioners' sugar and 2 tablespoons Jack Daniel's Whiskey. Makes 6 to 7 dozen.

OL' SOUTH PRALINES

2 cups sugar
1 teaspoon baking soda
1 cup buttermilk
⅛ teaspoon salt
2 tablespoons butter
2½ cups pecan halves
¼ cup Jack Daniel's Whiskey
1 teaspoon vanilla

Combine sugar, soda, buttermilk and salt in a heavy saucepan. Using a candy thermometer, cook until mixture reaches 210°, stirring constantly. Add butter and pecans. Continue cooking and stirring until thermometer reaches 235°. Remove from heat; add Jack Daniel's Whiskey and vanilla. Beat by hand until candy begins to thicken. Form candy into patties by dropping from a spoon onto a greased surface. Wrap individually in waxed paper. Store in airtight containers. Makes 3 dozen.

Tennessee Walking Horses

Tennessee is known all over the globe for its beautiful and famous Walking Horses. In size, color, and general appearance, the Tennessee Walking Horse may look similar to other saddle horses, but in its gaits and strides, nodding its head with every step, the Walking Horse is unmistakable.

Never was there a flashier colored horse. Satiny black, pure white, brown, roan, bay, or chestnut, the horses are beautiful to behold. But as good as a champion Walking Horse looks standing in the ring, it is his distinctive gait, called a running walk, that sets the Walking Horse apart from other breeds. The running walk has made the Walking Horse the favored saddle horse of pleasure horsemen and has added spectacular crowd appeal to show rings. "Riding a good horse," says one trainer, "is better than riding in a Lincoln Continental. He just floats along."

In the running walk, the horse carries his head low. The running walk is an extremely fast and gliding version of the flat-footed walk.

Manners are also an important consideration in showing horses. A well-mannered horse shows with brilliance and enthusiasm, executes the commands of the ringmaster at the touch of his rider. Tennessee Walking Horses have a quiet and even temperament. They are easy to handle and easy to ride, which makes them good and natural show horses.

Every year since 1939, Shelbyville, a few miles up the road from Lynchburg, has hosted the ten-day National Walking Horse Celebration. In the years past, horses such as Strolling Jim, Merry Go Boy, Midnight Sun, and Talk of the Town took the championships. Today, groomed and pampered champions command stud fees of $1,000 and up, and horses sell for more than a quarter of a million dollars.

Tennessee Walking Horses, like the people in the state for which they are named, are colorful, beautiful, distinctive, and genteel.

ADULT CHRISTMAS TREATS

2 cups pecans
2 cups vanilla wafer crumbs
2 cups sifted confectioners' sugar
¼ cup cocoa
    Pinch of salt
3 tablespoons white corn syrup
¼ cup plus 2 tablespoons Jack Daniel's Whiskey
    Confectioners' sugar, sifted

Toast pecans in a 300° oven until lightly browned (do not overcook as nuts tend to darken and become crisper as they cool); chop. Combine crumbs, pecans, sugar, cocoa and salt. Stir together Jack Daniel's Whiskey and corn syrup; combine with crumb mixture. Shape into balls using one tablespoon each. Roll in confectioners' sugar. Makes 6 to 7 dozen.

TRUFFLES

8 ounces (8 squares) semi-sweet chocolate, melted
1 stick butter, softened
1½ tablespoons Jack Daniel's Whiskey
⅔ cup finely crushed ginger snaps or graham cracker
    crumbs
    Cocoa
    Sugar

Combine first 4 ingredients; blend well. Cool in refrigerator until firm. Form 1 tablespoonful of mixture at a time into balls; roll in mixture of cocoa and sugar. Makes 2 dozen.

PECAN CHEWS

4 eggs, well beaten
1 16-ounce box light brown sugar
2 cups all-purpose flour
2 teaspoons baking powder
1 teaspoon salt
1 cup chopped pecans
1 teaspoon vanilla

Preheat oven to 300°. Combine eggs with brown sugar in top of double boiler; stir until sugar is dissolved. Add the remaining ingredients; mix well. Spread in shallow 15x10-inch pan and bake for about 25 minutes. Cool and cut into squares. Makes 2 dozen.

APPLE 'LASSES ICE CREAM

2 cups half-and-half
¼ cup firmly packed dark brown sugar
½ cup sugar
    Pinch of salt
1 tablespoon molasses
3 eggs, beaten
1 cup heavy cream
1 cup peeled, cored and finely chopped apples
½ teaspoon vanilla

Combine half-and-half, sugars, salt and molasses in a saucepan. Simmer over medium heat until slightly thickened, stirring often. Slowly stir a small amount of mixture into eggs; then add eggs to cream mixture and continue cooking for several minutes. Remove from heat and cool to room temperature. Fold in cream, apples and vanilla. Chill in refrigerator first, then freeze in an ice cream freezer. This is especially good over apple pie. Makes 1 quart.

GLACE AUX RAISINS
AND JACK DANIEL'S
(Raisins and Jack Daniel's Ice Cream)

2 cups milk
2 cups heavy cream
14 egg yolks
¾ cup sugar
    Dash salt
1 cup raisins
½ cup Jack Daniel's Whiskey
¼ teaspoon finely grated lemon peel

Scald milk and cream in heavy saucepan. (Tiny bubbles should form around the edge of the pan.) In bowl, whisk yolks, sugar and salt. Gradually stir a little of the hot milk into yolks. (It is easier to do these steps in the blender: while beating egg yolk mixture, slowly add all the hot liquid, then return mixture to saucepan.) Stir over medium heat until mixture coats spoon. Pour into bowl; cool completely. Cover and chill overnight. Combine raisins and Jack Daniel's Whiskey in small bowl. Cover; set aside overnight. Next day, combine custard mixture, raisin mixture and lemon peel. Churn-freeze in hand crank or electric ice-cream maker according to manufacturer's directions. (Though ice-cream maker gives best results, it is possible to make in freezer. When partially frozen, beat with electric mixer. Ripen in freezer for several hours.) Makes about 2 quarts.

NEVER ON SUNDAY CHOCOLATE ICE CREAM

2 cups heavy cream
2 cups half-and-half
⅔ cup sugar
⅓ cup unsweetened cocoa
2½ ounces semi-sweet chocolate, coarsely chopped
6 eggs, well beaten
½ cup Jack Daniel's Whiskey

Bring cream and half-and-half to a simmer in large heavy saucepan. Add sugar and cocoa; stir until sugar dissolves. Remove from heat. Add chocolate; stir until smooth. Gradually whisk ½ cup chocolate mixture into eggs. Return mixture to saucepan. Stir over medium-low heat for 10 to 15 minutes or until mixture thickens and coats back of spoon. Strain into bowl; cool completely, stirring often. Stir whiskey into custard. Pour custard into 1-quart ice cream churn; freeze according to manufacturer's directions. Store in a covered container for several hours to mellow flavor. If ice cream is frozen solid, soften in refrigerator before serving. Makes 1 quart.

JACK DANIEL'S ICE CREAM

1 medium bottle maraschino cherries or crystallized cherries
2 cups chopped pecans
½ cup Jack Daniel's Whiskey
½ gallon vanilla ice cream
1 dozen stale macaroons, crumbled

Soak cherries and nuts in Jack Daniel's Whiskey overnight. Remove ice cream from carton. Soften just enough to fold in whiskey mixture and macaroons. Return to large container and refreeze. Mixture will be softer than regular ice cream because of the whiskey. Makes 12 to 14 servings.

LEMON SPONGE CUSTARD

Grated rind from 1 lemon
Juice of 1 lemon
2 tablespoons butter, softened
1 cup sugar
4 tablespoons all-purpose flour
⅛ teaspoon salt
3 eggs, separated
1½ cups milk

Preheat oven to 350°. Grate rind from whole lemon, then juice lemon. Cream the butter. Add sugar, flour, salt and lemon juice. Beat the egg yolks; add milk. Blend well. Combine with flour mixture. Beat egg whites until stiff and fold in. Add lemon rind; stir. Pour into buttered baking dish (or custard cups) and set into larger baking pan. Pour hot tap water into pan around custard dish or cups. Bake for 40 to 45 minutes or until set. Makes 4 servings.

CHOCOLATE WHISKEY CHARLOTTE

Ladyfingers, split
1 14-ounce can sweetened condensed milk
1 6-ounce package semi-sweet chocolate morsels
3 tablespoons Jack Daniel's Whiskey
1 cup heavy cream, whipped

Line bottom of 2-quart charlotte mold or spring-form pan with waxed paper. Arrange split ladyfingers in design on bottom and along sides. Combine milk and chocolate in double boiler over simmering water. Stir until chocolate is melted. Remove from heat; cool completely. Add Jack Daniel's Whiskey; fold in whipped cream, reserving some for garnish. Gently pour into dish lined with ladyfingers. Cover filling with remaining ladyfingers. Cover and freeze 8 hours or overnight. Unmold and garnish with reserved whipped cream. Makes 10 to 12 servings.

Tart Strawberry Mousse

¼ cup orange juice
1 envelope unflavored gelatin
2 cups strawberries
4 tablespoons sugar or to taste
1 cup sour cream
  Whole strawberries

Sprinkle the gelatin over the orange juice in a small saucepan. Wash and hull the strawberries and purée in a food processor fitted with a steel blade. Add the sugar. Heat the orange juice and gelatin over low heat until the gelatin is dissolved; add to the strawberries. Blend in sour cream. Pour mousse into 6 individual soufflé dishes or stemmed wine glasses. Refrigerate several hours before serving. Garnish with whole strawberries. Makes 6 servings.

Frozen Tennessee Chocolate Mousse

1 6-ounce package semi-sweet chocolate morsels
¼ cup water
1 tablespoon honey
½ teaspoon salt
2 tablespoons Jack Daniel's Whiskey
½ cup ground pecans (use food processor or blender)
2 eggs whites
½ cup sugar
1½ cups heavy cream, divided
1 teaspoon vanilla
¼ cup brown sugar
  Pecan halves

Melt the chocolate in a small saucepan with water, honey and salt. Remove from the heat; stir in Jack Daniel's Whiskey and pecans. In a bowl, beat the egg whites until stiff. Gradually beat in ½ cup sugar until mixture is thick and glossy. Gently fold in the chocolate mixture. In a separate bowl, beat 1 cup heavy cream with vanilla until thick. Gradually beat in the brown sugar. Spread one-third

of the chocolate mixture into an attractive, 1½-quart serving bowl. Cover with half the whipped cream mixture. Repeat layers, ending with a layer of chocolate. Cover bowl; freeze for at least 6 hours, preferably overnight. Just before serving, whip the remaining ½ cup heavy cream and pipe onto mousse in an attractive pattern. Garnish with pecan halves. (Recipe may be doubled.) Makes 6 to 8 servings.

Johnny Appleseed Pudding

1 cup sugar
1 egg
2 tablespoons all-purpose flour
¼ teaspoon cinnamon
¼ teaspoon nutmeg
1 teaspoon baking powder
  Pinch of salt
3 medium cooking apples, peeled, cored and chopped
½ cup chopped nuts
  Whipped cream

Preheat oven to 350°. In an electric mixer, beat sugar and egg until frothy. Combine flour, spices, baking powder and salt. Stir into sugar mixture. Fold in apples and nuts. Pour into a buttered 9-inch pie pan. Bake for 20 to 25 minutes or until crusty and brown. Serve warm with whipped cream. Makes 6 servings.

Glorious Sweet Potato Pudding

3 cups sweet potatoes, cooked and mashed
½ cup sugar
2 eggs, beaten
¼ cup Jack Daniel's Whiskey
⅓ cup milk
½ cup butter, melted
1 cup firmly packed light brown sugar
¼ cup all-purpose flour
1 cup pecans, chopped
¼ cup butter, melted

Preheat oven to 350°. Combine potatoes, sugar, eggs, Jack Daniel's Whiskey, milk and butter. Spread into 9x13-inch baking dish. Combine remaining ingredients; sprinkle over potatoes. Bake for 25 to 30 minutes. Makes 10 servings.

Old Maid's Sweet Potato Pudding

¼ cup butter
½ cup sugar
¼ cup firmly packed light brown sugar
2 eggs, beaten
1 teaspoon cinnamon
¼ teaspoon nutmeg
¼ teaspoon cloves
   Dash of salt
2½ cups shredded uncooked sweet potatoes
1½ cups milk
   Whipped cream

Preheat oven to 400°. Cream butter and sugars; beat eggs into sugar mixture. Add spices and salt. Stir potatoes into sugar mixture; add milk and mix thoroughly. Pour into a greased 2-quart baking dish. Bake 50 to 60 minutes. Serve topped with whipped cream. Makes 6 to 8 servings.

Bread Pudding with Tennessee Whiskey Sauce

6 cups cubed, stale French or Italian bread
1 apple, peeled, cored and grated
1 cup raisins
3 large eggs
1 cup sugar
2 cups milk
1 teaspoon vanilla
½ teaspoon nutmeg
   Pinch of salt
   Butter
   Tennessee Whiskey Sauce

Combine bread, apple and raisins. Set aside. Beat eggs until frothy; beat in sugar. Add milk, vanilla, nutmeg and salt. Pour over bread mixture; set aside for 15 minutes for bread to soak up liquid. Preheat oven to 375°. Generously butter a 1½-quart casserole. Pour bread mixture into dish; place in a larger pan in the oven. Pour boiling water into the outer pan to a depth of 1 inch. Bake for 40 to 45 minutes or until tester inserted in center comes out almost clean. Prepare and serve Tennessee Whiskey Sauce with warm pudding. Makes 8 servings.

TENNESSEE WHISKEY SAUCE

    1¼ cups water
    ½ cup firmly packed light brown sugar
    ¼ teaspoon nutmeg
    ¼ cup Jack Daniel's Whiskey
    1½ tablespoons cornstarch
    2 tablespoons butter

Combine water, sugar and nutmeg in a saucepan. Bring to a boil. Combine Jack Daniel's Whiskey and cornstarch; stir into sugar mixture. Cook until thickened. Blend in butter until melted. Makes 1¾ cups.

STRAWBERRIES WITH STRAWBERRY SAUCE

    5 cups capped fresh, whole strawberries
    ½ cup frozen orange juice concentrate
    ¼ cup white wine
    2 tablespoons sugar
    Mint sprigs

In a food processor with the steel blade, purée ⅓ of the strawberries with the orange juice concentrate, wine and sugar. Halve the remaining strawberries and divide among 4 stemmed wine glasses. Pour sauce over berries; top each with a sprig of mint. Makes 4 servings.

APPLE GOODIE

    3 or 4 apples, thinly sliced
    1 tablespoon all-purpose flour
    ¼ teaspoon salt
    1 cup sugar
    ½ teaspoon cinnamon
    ¾ cup uncooked oats
    ¾ cup all-purpose flour
    ¾ cup firmly packed brown sugar
    ¼ teaspoon baking powder
    ¼ teaspoon baking soda
    1 stick butter

Mix the first 5 ingredients and place in buttered baking dish. Combine remaining ingredients, except butter, and pour over apples. Melt butter; pour over all. Bake for 30 minutes at 350°. Makes 4 servings.

SWEDISH CREAM WITH FRESH FRUIT

    1 envelope unflavored gelatin
    1 cup heavy cream
    1 cup sugar
    1 cup sour cream
    ½ teaspoon almond extract
    Sweetened fresh fruit: strawberries, blueberries and/ or peaches

In a small saucepan, sprinkle gelatin on cream to soften for several minutes. Stir in sugar; heat until gelatin and sugar are dissolved. Remove from heat and chill until mixture begins to thicken. Add sour cream and almond extract; stir until smooth. Pour into a 3-cup mold that has been rinsed with cold water. Chill until firm. Unmold and serve topped with sweetened fresh fruit. Makes 4 to 6 servings.

Miss Mary Bobo's Boarding House Gingerbread with Lemon Sauce

1 cup molasses
½ cup sugar
½ cup butter, softened
½ cup boiling water
1 egg, beaten
1 teaspoon baking soda
1 teaspoon cinnamon
1 teaspoon ground ginger
½ teaspoon ground allspice
½ teaspoon salt
3 cups all-purpose flour
Lemon Sauce

Preheat oven to 350°. With an electric mixer combine molasses and sugar. Add butter; slowly add boiling water; mix well. Stir in egg. Combine dry ingredients; add to molasses mixture. Pour batter into a greased and floured 9x13-inch baking pan. Bake for 25 to 30 minutes or until cake springs back when lightly touched in the center. Cool in pan. To serve, cut into squares and top with Lemon Sauce. Makes 15 to 18 servings

LEMON SAUCE

1 tablespoon cornstarch
½ cup sugar
Dash of salt
1 cup boiling water
2 tablespoons lemon juice
1 teaspoon lemon rind, grated

Mix cornstarch, sugar and salt. Stir in boiling water. Bring to a boil, stirring constantly; cook until thickened. Remove from heat; add lemon juice and rind; mix well.

UNCLE JACK'S FAVORITE DESSERT

6 tablespoons butter
¼ cup firmly packed light brown sugar
½ cup sugar
⅓ cup water
6 ripe peaches, peeled, halved and pitted
⅓ cup Jack Daniel's Whiskey
Whipped cream

Melt butter. Add sugars and stir until dissolved. Stir in water. Add peach halves and simmer, turning often, for 20 to 25 minutes. Pour Jack Daniel's Whiskey over the peaches and carefully ignite. When flame dies, serve halves topped with syrup and a spoon of whipped cream. Makes 6 servings.

PEACHES AND CREAM

1 cup firmly packed light brown sugar
1 cup sour cream
1 cup heavy cream, whipped
8 ripe peaches, peeled and thinly sliced
⅓ cup cookie crumbs

Combine the brown sugar and sour cream until the sugar has dissolved. Fold in the whipped cream. Just before serving, fold in the peach slices. Serve in stemmed glasses topped with cookie crumbs. Makes 8 servings.

SPIKED PEACH SAUCE

2 cups sliced peaches
5 tablespoons brown sugar
2 tablespoons butter
¼ cup Jack Daniel's Whiskey

Combine all ingredients in saucepan over low heat. Stir until sugar melts. Serve over pound cake or ice cream. Makes 2 cups.

DATE SQUARES

1 pound dates, pitted and chopped
¾ cup sugar
1 cup water
¼ cup Jack Daniel's Whiskey
½ cup butter
1 cup firmly packed brown sugar
1½ cups all-purpose flour
1 teaspoon baking soda
½ teaspoon salt
1¾ cups quick-cooking oats
1 tablespoon Jack Daniel's Whiskey

Combine first 4 ingredients; cook over low heat, stirring constantly, about 10 minutes or until thickened. Cool. Preheat oven to 350°. Grease an 8x8x2-inch baking pan. Cream butter and brown sugar; combine flour, baking soda, salt and oats. Add dry ingredients to butter mixture. Stir in Jack Daniel's Whiskey. Press half the mixture into bottom of baking pan. Spread with date filling. Top with remaining crumb mixture, pressing lightly. Bake 25 to 30 minutes or until lightly browned. Cut into bars when lightly cooled. Makes 2 dozen.

CARAMELIZED FRESH FRUIT DESSERT

Green seedless grapes, strawberries, raspberries or peaches
1 cup sour cream
2 teaspoons Jack Daniel's Whiskey
1 cup firmly packed light brown sugar

Fill an ovenproof shallow baking dish with a layer of one of the fruits. Combine sour cream with Jack Daniel's Whiskey. Cover fruit layer with cream mixture. Cover and refrigerate until thoroughly chilled. Just before serving, sprinkle cream layer with brown sugar to completely cover cream. Broil until sugar caramelizes. The sugar must dissolve but not scorch. Serve immediately.

BANANAS FLAMBÉ

3 tablespoons butter
⅓ cup firmly packed light brown sugar
Dash nutmeg
Dash cinnamon
3 firm bananas, split and halved
¼ cup Jack Daniel's Whiskey
Vanilla ice cream

Melt butter in large skillet over medium heat. Add sugar and spices; stir until melted. Place banana slices in skillet; cook until tender. Remove skillet from heat. Add Jack Daniel's Whiskey and carefully ignite. Serve hot over ice cream. Makes 6 servings.

MISS MARY'S FAMOUS BAKED APRICOT CASSEROLE

1 17-ounce can apricot halves, drained
1 cup firmly packed light brown sugar
1½ cups butter cracker crumbs (Ritz or Town House crackers)
½ cup butter

Preheat oven to 325°. Arrange apricots cut-side up in a greased casserole. Sprinkle brown sugar over apricots. Over this make a layer of cracker crumbs. Dot crumbs with butter. Bake for 35 to 40 minutes or until the casserole has thickened and is crusty on the top. Makes 4 to 6 servings.

PEACH SOUFFLÉ

1½ cups peeled and sliced fresh peaches
½ cup butter
½ cup sugar
5 eggs, separated
1 cup vanilla wafer crumbs
3 tablespoons Jack Daniel's Whiskey
   Pinch of salt

Preheat oven to 350°. Mash peach slices. Combine butter and sugar; beat until fluffy. Add egg yolks, one at a time, beating well after each addition. Stir in crumbs, Jack Daniel's Whiskey, salt and peaches. Whip egg whites until stiff; fold into peach mixture. Pour into buttered and sugared 7-inch soufflé dish and bake for 30 to 35 minutes or until set. Makes 6 servings.

PIATTO FORTE
(Italian Trifle)

Creation of Robert Franceschini, Memphis, Tennessee.

24 ladyfingers (48 halves)
3 ounces Jack Daniel's Whiskey
3 ounces light rum
1½ ounces vermouth
2 large packages vanilla pudding, prepared
½ pint heavy cream
   Red and green maraschino cherries, cut into halves

Place half the ladyfingers on bottom of platter. Combine Jack Daniel's Whiskey, rum and vermouth. Put ¼ teaspoon of combined liquor on each ladyfinger. Cover with vanilla pudding. Place the rest of the ladyfingers on top of custard. Put ½ teaspoon of combined liquor on each ladyfinger. Cover with vanilla pudding. Top with whipped cream; dot with a design of red and green cherries. Refrigerate for 2 hours and serve.

ALMOND MACAROON MOLD

The following dessert is a really spectacular ice cream mold flavored with Jack Daniel's. Ruth Daniel shared the recipe with a note attached: "You can adjust the flavoring according to taste, but I suggest another dessert if the preacher is coming."

3 dozen macaroons
   Jack Daniel's Whiskey
2 cups heavy cream, whipped
¼ cup sugar
2 quarts almond toffee ice cream (or English toffee)

Line a mold or silver bowl with 2½ dozen macaroons. Drizzle Jack Daniel's Whiskey over the macaroons. Cover bowl with foil and place in refrigerator to chill. Whip cream and gradually add sugar and 3 tablespoons Jack Daniel's Whiskey (or flavor as desired). Remove bowl from refrigerator and fill with ice cream. Smooth top. Spread whipped cream on top. Crumble remaining macaroons and sprinkle on top. Replace foil and place in freezer until serving time. Makes 8 servings.

TENNESSEE HOLLER-PUFF

12 ladyfingers, diced
¼ cup chopped walnuts
4 eggs
1¾ cups milk
⅛ teaspoon salt
¼ cup confectioners' sugar
¼ cup Jack Daniel's Whiskey
   Confectioners' sugar

Preheat oven to 350°. Grease a 1½-quart casserole dish. Spread ladyfingers over bottom. Sprinkle with nuts. Beat eggs in separate bowl, with remaining ingredients. Pour into casserole. Bake for 30 to 40 minutes, or until puffed and golden. Immediately, sprinkle top lightly with confectioners' sugar. Makes 6 servings.

RAISIN ROLL

Leola Dismukes is a retired cook from Miss Mary's Boarding House. Heavy handed when it came to spices, Leola created some wonderful desserts and spicy dishes. Much to Miss Mary's displeasure, however, she was fond of nutmeg and used it liberally in her cooking. Miss Mary told her she was going to sprinkle nutmeg on Leola's casket to keep Leola happy in eternity.

This spicy Raisin Roll doesn't have nutmeg, but it is rich in cinnamon . . . and delicious!

1 cup raisins
⅓ cup butter, melted
1 cup sugar
1 teaspoon cinnamon
½ cup pecans, chopped
1 9-inch pastry crust (use favorite recipe)
1 cup sugar
½ teaspoon baking soda
½ cup buttermilk
1 tablespoon white corn syrup
½ cup butter
¼ cup Jack Daniel's Whiskey

Plump raisins in enough boiling water to cover. Drain. Combine raisins, butter, sugar, cinnamon and pecans. Set aside. Preheat oven to 375°. Roll pastry into rectangular shape. Spread raisin filling evenly over entire surface. Roll pastry up (starting with a narrow side) jelly-roll style. Place on greased cookie sheet. Bake for 30 minutes or until golden brown. Slice to serve. Prepare sauce. Combine remaining ingredients, except Jack Daniel's Whiskey, in saucepan; cook over medium heat. Bring to a boil and continue boiling until soft-ball (235°) stage is reached. Remove from heat. Cool. Before serving, add Jack Daniel's Whiskey and stir. Pour over sliced raisin roll. Makes 8 to 10 servings.

DARING DATES

Pitted dates
Jack Daniel's Whiskey
Pecan halves, toasted
Sugar

Soak pitted dates in Jack Daniel's Whiskey overnight. Strain. Stuff toasted pecan into center of each date; roll in sugar. Store in airtight container.

BLACKBERRIES JUBILEE

2 cups fresh or frozen thawed blackberries
2 teaspoons cornstarch
2 tablespoons lemon juice
½ cup white grape juice
⅓ cup Jack Daniel's Whiskey, divided
Vanilla ice cream

Mash half the berries in saucepan. Dissolve cornstarch in lemon juice; add to berries along with grape juice and half the Jack Daniel's Whiskey. Heat until thickened and clear. Add remaining whole berries; warm. At the table, heat remaining Jack Daniel's Whiskey, pour over warm blackberries and carefully ignite. Ladle over ice cream. Makes 6 servings.

Old-Fashioned Pear Cobbler

Fall is an especially beautiful time in Lynchburg. The days are bright and crisp. It is a time for friends to chat about football games, fall planting, and school happenings. Visitors come to enjoy the extravagant color of our fall foliage.

The town square is a gathering place where whittling—a local pastime—is tried for the first time by many. Conversation is always friendly. The best part of the day in town, however, is the chance that one of the local restaurants is serving fresh pear cobbler with cream, the old-fashioned kind like grandmother served on crisp fall days.

5 firm pears, halved and cored
½ cup all-purpose flour
½ cup uncooked oats
Dash of salt
½ cup firmly packed brown sugar
¼ teaspoon each: cinnamon and nutmeg
½ cup butter
½ cup frozen limeade concentrate, thawed
Warm cream

Preheat oven to 375°. Arrange pears skin-side down in a greased baking dish. Combine flour, oats, sugar, salt, cinnamon and nutmeg. With a pastry cutter or fork, cut in butter until crumbly and well mixed. Pour limeade concentrate over pears, then sprinkle flour mixture over top. Bake for 30 minutes, or until pears are tender. Serve with warm cream. Makes 6 to 8 servings.

ALMOND STRAWBERRY MERINGUE

¾ cup almonds
3 large egg whites, at room temperature
¼ teaspoon cream of tartar
½ teaspoon almond extract
1 cup confectioners' sugar
2 cups topped and halved fresh strawberries
1 cup heavy cream, whipped
  Confectioners' sugar
  Whole strawberries

Roast almonds in a 325° oven for 10 to 15 minutes or until lightly brown. When cool, finely chop. Preheat oven to 225°. Beat egg whites in an electric mixer until foamy. Add cream of tartar and almond extract. Continue to beat; slowly add sugar one teaspoonful at a time until whites are stiff and glossy. Fold chopped almonds into meringue. Line two 8-inch cake pans with waxed paper. Divide meringue between the two pans. Bake for 1 hour. Do not remove from the oven at once, but turn off the oven, open the door and leave them for at least 5 minutes. Cool gradually, away from a draft. Remove from waxed paper when cool. Just before serving, fold strawberry halves into whipped cream. Place one meringue on a serving dish. Spread fruit mixture over this layer and top with the second meringue. Sprinkle with confectioners' sugar and several strawberry fans (take a beautiful uncapped berry and thinly slice from pointed end almost through to cap and fan out). Makes 6 servings.

AUNT LUTEY'S FROZEN DESSERT

¼ cup slivered almonds
¼ cup toasted coconut
½ pint whipping cream

¼ cup plus 2 tablespoons sugar
1 teaspoon instant coffee powder
1 egg white, whipped

Mix almonds and coconut. Whip cream; gradually add ¼ cup sugar and instant coffee. Beat egg white until stiff and add remaining 2 tablespoons of sugar. Fold egg white into whipped cream mixture. Gradually fold in half of coconut/almond mixture. Place paper liners in 12 muffin cups; spoon mixture into liners. Top with remaining coconut/almond mixture and place in the freezer until ready to serve. Makes 12 servings.

MINT JULEP BAVARIAN

Created by Executive Chef Robert Siegel, Maude's Courtyard, Nashville, Tennessee.

2 cups milk
8 egg yolks
1½ cups sugar
2 envelopes unflavored gelatin
½ cup Jack Daniel's Whiskey
2 teaspoons spearmint extract or flavoring
2 cups heavy cream
  Mint sprigs
  Whipped cream

In the top of a double boiler over simmering water, combine cold milk, egg yolks and sugar. Heat over simmering water, stirring constantly, until the custard mixture is hot and steamy and thick enough to coat the spoon. Remove from heat. Mix the gelatin in a glass with the Jack Daniel's Whiskey and spearmint extract. Add to the custard, mixing thoroughly. Cool custard to lukewarm, stirring occasionally. Whip the cream until stiff; fold into the custard. Pour into serving glasses or molds and refrigerate for several hours. Unmold and garnish with a mint sprig and whipped cream. Makes 4 servings.

FAMILY-SIZED STRAWBERRY SHORTCAKE

Few desserts can beat old-fashioned strawberry shortcake. Since strawberries grow in abundance in Tennessee, especially in Portland, up near the Kentucky state line, it stands to reason that they are served up in nigh on a thousand different ways. Here is a wonderful new shortcake as big as a pizza. In fact, you cook the shortcake (one family size) on a pizza pan. Diane Overstreet says that her mother cooks this for their family get-togethers.

1 cup all-purpose flour
1 stick butter
¼ cup confectioners' sugar

½ cup sugar
2 3-ounce packages cream cheese, softened
½ teaspoon vanilla
½ cup strawberry slices
1 cup crushed strawberries
4 tablespoons sugar
1 tablespoon cornstarch

Preheat oven to 325°. Mix together flour, butter and confectioners' sugar; mash onto a 13-inch pizza pan. Bake for 20 minutes. Cool. Beat sugar, cream cheese and vanilla until fluffy. Spread over crust. Cover filling with strawberry slices. Combine remaining ingredients in saucepan; cook until clear and thickened. Pour over berries very slowly. Chill until set and ENJOY! Makes 6 to 8 servings.

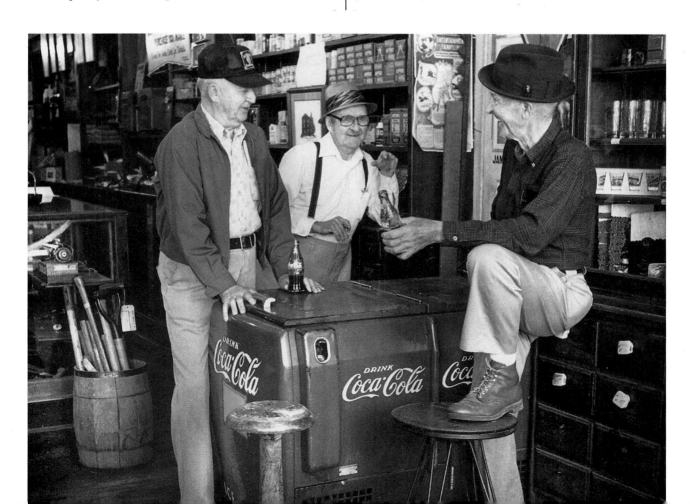

The Lynchburg Hardware and General Store

I f the ravages of time have caught any one establishment in its fast movement, it would have to be the local hardware and general store. Every time a settlement would spring up in a vale or a hollow in Tennessee, just about the first business to open its doors would be the general store. The general store was to the local citizens what our newspaper, meeting house, post office, fast food restaurant and entertainment centers are to us today.

These stores carried everything from onion sets to union suits. The post office was postage stamp size. Checkers played with soda pop caps on a homemade checkerboard went on all day. Fast foods were crackers, mustard and bologna washed down with a "country red" or maybe a "big orange" soda pop. A screen door with fly-paper dangling slammed in the summertime and a potbellied stove warmed visitors in the winter. News of meetings, engagements, new births or sickness was passed along with any "outside" (the county, that is) news of general interest.

Few of these general stores are left today, but they are rich to visit. Lynchburg has a general store with shelves full of green salve and mustard plaster, hunting knives and fishing lures, hogwashers and longjohns, shoestrings and nails and a few hundred other things.

There is a Coke cooler where you can still get a 10¢ Coke. The checkerboard sits on a barrel ready for anyone who might saunter in for a game or two. Rocking chairs are filled with the local philosophers, some whittling, some rocking. The potbellied stove is at the back with the coffin that a man returned. He wanted to choose his own casket, so he ordered two. He made his choice and then returned the second.

Next time you're in the area, why don't you drop in, bring your whittling knife or join the checker players, have a 10¢ Coke and cool your heels in Lynchburg's general store. Besides you might find something you've been needing, like gold embroidery needles, tuxedo overalls, or the finest handmade hunting knife.

GERMAN CHOCOLATE UPSIDE-DOWN CAKE

Not many people can lay claim to the fact that they run a saloon in a dry county and the strongest drink on the menu is root beer. But Marie Clark does. Marie runs the White Rabbit Saloon and Restaurant in Lynchburg. The establishment still sports the old serving bar, back bar and mirror, and the multiple fans all turned by one motor from its earlier and more colorful past. Today Marie and the staff serve up Tennessee pull-pork barbecue, chili, sandwiches, and desserts with assorted soft drinks. Pretty tame stuff, but good eating.

Marie shared her recipe for German Chocolate Upside Down Cake. Sort of like the saloon, it appears different than it is . . . and well worth trying when you're in the mood for a sweet.

1 box German chocolate cake mix
1 cup chopped pecans
1 8-ounce package cream cheese, softened
1 stick butter, softened
1 box confectioners' sugar
1½ cups coconut

Preheat oven to 350°. Grease a 9x13-inch cake pan. Prepare cake mix as directed on package. Stir in nuts and pour batter into pan. Blend cream cheese and butter. Add confectioners' sugar and coconut. Drop by teaspoonsful on top of raw cake batter (mixture is very thick) until coconut mixture is all used up. Bake for 45 to 50 minutes. The cake batter rises and the coconut-cream cheese mixture settles to bottom. This is a delicious, moist cheesecake-like dessert. Makes 10-12 servings.

WHISKEY SOUR PARFAIT

1 envelope unflavored gelatin
1 cup sugar, divided
¼ teaspoon salt
½ cup lemon juice
¼ cup orange juice
5 slightly beaten egg yolks
¼ cup Jack Daniel's Whiskey
5 egg whites
Grated orange peel
Orange slices
Maraschino cherries

In saucepan, mix gelatin, ⅔ cup sugar and salt. Stir in lemon juice, orange juice and egg yolks. Cook and stir until slightly thickened. Remove from heat and stir in whiskey. Chill until thickness of corn syrup; stir occasionally to blend. Immediately beat egg whites to soft peak stage. Gradually add remaining ⅓ cup sugar and beat until stiff peaks form. Fold in stiffly beaten egg whites. Chill until mixture mounds when spooned into parfait glasses. Chill several hours or overnight. Garnish with orange peel, orange slice and stemmed maraschino cherry. Makes 6 servings.

CAKES & PIES

Aunt Pittypat's Pecan Pound Cake

>   1 cup solid vegetable shortening
> 2½ cups sugar
>   6 eggs
>   3 cups sifted cake flour
>   2 teaspoons baking powder
>   1 teaspoon salt
>   ½ teaspoon nutmeg
>   1 cup sour cream
>   ½ cup Jack Daniel's Whiskey
>   1 cup finely chopped pecans
>   Gone With The Wind Glaze

Preheat oven to 325°. Grease and flour a 10-inch tube pan or Bundt pan. In large mixer bowl, beat shortening and sugar until light and fluffy; add eggs, one at a time, beating until very smooth. Sift flour, baking powder, salt and nutmeg; add to sugar mixture alternately with sour cream and Jack Daniel's Whiskey, beginning and ending with flour. Beat just until well blended; fold in pecans. Turn into prepared pan. Bake for 1 hour and 15 minutes or until a tester inserted in center comes out clean. Cool in pan 15 minutes, then turn out on a wire rack and finish cooling. Pour glaze over cake, decorate with pecan halves, if desired.

Gone With The Wind Glaze

>   2 cups confectioners' sugar
>   1 tablespoon Jack Daniel's Whiskey

Mix confectioners' sugar, Jack Daniel's Whiskey and enough water (about 2 tablespoons) to make a pourable glaze; beat until very smooth. Pour over cake.

JACK DANIEL'S CHOCOLATE VELVET CAKE

This cake is a very deep dark smooth chocolate lover's dream. It was created by Executive Chef Robert Siegel, Maude's Courtyard, Nashville, Tennessee.

1 8-inch diameter sponge cake, 1-inch thick
2 ounces Jack Daniel's Whiskey, divided
2 pounds semi-sweet chocolate
1 cup heavy cream
6 egg whites
¼ cup sugar
Whipped cream

Place sponge cake layer in the bottom of a spring-form pan and douse the sponge with 1 ounce of Jack Daniel's Whiskey. Set aside. Place the chocolate, broken into pieces, into the top of a double boiler over simmering water; add 1 ounce of Jack Daniel's Whiskey and heat, stirring until the chocolate is smooth and fully melted. Whip the heavy cream until stiff peaks form. Beat the egg whites until stiff peaks form, adding sugar a little at a time until all is used. Fold the whipped cream, chocolate, and egg whites together. Mix thoroughly, but not vigorously. Pour the chocolate mixture into the cake-lined pan; refrigerate overnight. Remove cake from pan and smooth the sides with a cake spatula. Decorate the borders with whipped cream.

Note: Any sponge cake can be used, either commercial or homemade. A quick genoise (fine French sponge cake) can be made by mixing 4 whole eggs

in a stainless mixing bowl with ½ cup granulated sugar. Place the bowl in warm water until the egg mixture is lukewarm. Grease and flour an 8-inch cake pan. Melt ½ stick butter and set aside. With an electric mixer, whip the egg mixture for 10 minutes on high speed until it is light yellow in color and very thick. Fold in ½ cup sifted flour, then add melted butter. Mix gently but thoroughly. Pour the batter into the pan and bake for 15 minutes at 350°. Remove from pan and cool.

PLANTATION CAKE

1½ cups sifted all-purpose flour
1 teaspoon baking powder
½ teaspoon salt
1½ cups finely chopped pecans (about 5 ounces)
1 stick unsalted butter, softened
1¾ cups plus 2 tablespoons sugar, divided
¼ cup Jack Daniel's Whiskey mixed with ½ cup water
4 egg whites
1 ounce unsweetened chocolate, coarsely chopped
2 cups heavy cream
2 teaspoons vanilla
¼ cup confectioners' sugar, sifted
1 teaspoon cocoa

Preheat the oven to 375°. Grease two 8-inch round cake pans; line the bottoms with waxed paper. Grease the paper and then lightly flour the pans; tap out any excess. In a medium bowl, sift together the flour, baking powder and salt. Add the pecans; mix well. In a large bowl, cream the butter and 1½ cups of the sugar with an electric mixer until light and fluffy. Add the flour mixture, ¼ at a time, alternately with the diluted whiskey, beginning and ending with the flour. Mix well after each addition. In a large bowl, beat the egg whites until stiff but not dry. Gently fold egg whites into the batter ⅓ cup at a time. Fold in the remaining egg whites. Pour into the prepared pans. Bake the cakes for 20 to 25 minutes, or until a tester inserted in the center comes out clean. Cool for about 10 minutes; then run a knife around the edges and unmold onto a rack. Cool. In a small heavy saucepan, combine the chocolate, ¼ cup of the remaining sugar and 2 tablespoons of the heavy cream. Cook over moderate heat, stirring, until the chocolate is melted and mixture is smooth. Remove from heat and whisk until cooled. Add ¼ cup sifted confectioners' sugar to remaining cream. Beat cream until fairly stiff. Divide into 2 parts. Place half the cream in a separate bowl. Fold cooled chocolate mixture and 1 teaspoon vanilla into one bowl of whipped cream until blended. Whisk remaining 2 tablespoons sugar and 1 teaspoon vanilla into the other. Cover both bowls and refrigerate until ready to use. Pile chocolate whipped cream onto one layer of cake and top with second layer. Frost top and sides with vanilla cream. Sprinkle the cocoa over the top. Refrigerate, lightly covered with wax paper, for up to one day before serving. Makes 8 to 10 servings.

BLACK BOTTOM CUPCAKES

   1 8-ounce package cream cheese, softened
   1 egg, beaten
   ⅓ cup sugar
   ⅛ teaspoon salt
   1 cup semi-sweet chocolate morsels
1½ cups all-purpose flour
   1 cup sugar
   ¼ cup cocoa
   ½ teaspoon cinnamon
   1 teaspoon baking soda
   ½ teaspoon salt
   ¼ cup Jack Daniel's Whiskey
   ¾ cup water
   ⅓ cup vegetable oil
   1 tablespoon vinegar
   1 teaspoon vanilla

Preheat oven to 350°. Line muffin tins with paper cupcake liners. Combine first 4 ingredients. Stir in chocolate morsels. Set aside. Combine remaining dry ingredients in separate bowl. Stir together Jack Daniel's Whiskey, water, oil, vinegar and vanilla; add to dry ingredients. Fill cupcake liners ¾ full with batter. Drop 1 tablespoon cream cheese mixture into center of each. Bake 35 to 40 minutes or until tester inserted in center comes out almost clean. Makes 18 cupcakes.

COCONUT POUND CAKE

   1 cup butter or shortening
   2 cups sugar
   5 eggs
   1 teaspoon coconut extract
   2 cups all-purpose flour
1½ teaspoons baking powder
   1 teaspoon salt
   1 cup buttermilk
   1 cup shredded coconut
   1 cup sugar
   ½ cup water
   1 teaspoon coconut extract

Preheat oven to 350°. Cream butter and sugar. Add eggs, one at a time, beating two minutes after each addition; add extract. Combine next 3 ingredients; add alternately with buttermilk to the egg mixture. Stir in coconut. Pour batter into greased 10-inch tube pan and bake for 50 to 60 minutes. To make glaze, combine remaining ingredients; boil for 2 minutes. Pour over warm cake. Makes 10 to 12 servings.

UNCLE JACK'S FAVORITE APPLESAUCE CAKE

   ½ cup butter
   2 eggs
   1 cup firmly packed light brown sugar
2½ cups sifted all-purpose flour
   2 teaspoons baking soda
   ¼ teaspoon salt
   ½ teaspoon cinnamon
   ½ teaspoon ground cloves
   ¼ cup wheat germ
   2 cups sweetened applesauce
   ¼ cup Jack Daniel's Whiskey
   1 cup English walnuts, chopped

Preheat oven to 325°. Have all ingredients at room temperature. Grease and flour a 9x5x3-inch loaf pan. Cream butter, eggs and sugar in mixer. Combine flour, soda, salt, spices and wheat germ; add to egg mixture. Stir in applesauce, Jack Daniel's Whiskey and nuts. Pour into pan and bake for 55 to 60 minutes or until tester inserted in center comes out clean. Cool and remove from pan. *Optional ingredients:* add 1 cup raisins or 1 cup chopped dates or both when stirring in nuts. Makes 1 loaf cake.

PEACH MERINGUE CAKE

   ½ cup butter, softened
   ½ cup sugar

4 egg yolks
⅔ cup cake flour
1 teaspoon baking powder
¼ teaspoon salt
¼ cup milk
4 egg whites
¾ cup sugar
1 teaspoon vanilla
¾ cup pecans, chopped
  Sliced peaches
  Whipped cream

Preheat oven to 325°. Grease and flour two 8-inch round cake pans. Cream butter and sugar with mixer; add egg yolks and mix thoroughly. Combine flour, baking powder and salt. Add dry ingredients to egg mixture alternately with milk. Pour into cake pans. Set aside while preparing meringue. Beat egg whites until foamy, but not dry. Gradually add sugar by the tablespoonful until all is used. Add vanilla. Divide meringue and spread over *unbaked* cake batter. Sprinkle with nuts. Bake 20 to 25 minutes, being careful not to overbake. Cool. Cut into wedges to serve. Top with sweetened, sliced peaches. Garnish with whipped cream. Makes 6 to 8 servings.

BLACK LABEL FUDGE CAKE

It makes a fudge sauce as it bakes!

1 tablespoon butter
1½ cups unsifted all-purpose flour
¾ cup sugar
1 tablespoon baking powder
4 tablespoons cocoa, divided
¾ cup milk
1¼ teaspoons vanilla
¾ cup chopped walnuts
½ cup firmly packed brown sugar
¼ cup Jack Daniel's Whiskey
⅓ cup cold water
  Whipped cream or ice cream

Preheat oven to 325°. Place butter in 8x8-inch baking pan; melt in oven. Remove from oven; set aside. In a medium bowl, combine flour, sugar, baking powder and 2 tablespoons cocoa. Blend in milk and vanilla. Stir in nuts. Spread into pan with melted butter. Evenly sprinkle batter with brown sugar, mixed with remaining 2 tablespoons of cocoa. Pour whiskey and cold water evenly over top of cake. Bake 20 to 25 minutes, or until cake is firm with a fudgy sauce on top. Serve warm with whipped cream or ice cream. Makes 4 to 6 servings.

BLACK JACK CAKE

¼ cup black walnuts
1 box butter recipe chocolate cake mix
1 stick butter
4 eggs, slightly beaten
½ cup black coffee
½ cup Jack Daniel's Whiskey
1 stick butter
1 16-ounce box confectioners' sugar
3 teaspoons cocoa
⅓ cup creme de cacao liqueur
1 teaspoon vanilla
  Black walnut pieces

Preheat oven to 350°. Grease a fluted torte pan (or bundt pan). Sprinkle the black walnuts evenly on bottom of pan. Set aside. Blend next 5 ingredients together until smooth. Pour batter into prepared pan. Bake for 45 to 50 minutes or until tester inserted in center comes out clean. Place on rack to cool. To make frosting, place butter in saucepan on very low heat and melt (do not brown). Add sugar, cocoa and liqueur. Stir until blended and frosting becomes glossy. Add vanilla. Pour frosting on cake. Sprinkle top with broken black walnuts. Makes 10 to 12 servings.

BRIDESMAID CAKE

1 box white cake mix
3 egg whites
⅓ cup vegetable oil
½ cup water
¾ cup Bols Triple Sec liqueur
½ teaspoon minced orange peel
1 stick butter
1 16-ounce box confectioners' sugar
3 teaspoons Bols Orange Curacao
½ cup broken walnuts
¼ cup candied ginger, optional
½ teaspoon minced orange peel

Preheat oven to 350°. Mix first 6 ingredients until batter is smooth and creamy. Pour batter into a greased and slightly floured 9x13-inch cake pan. Bake for 30 to 35 minutes, or until tester inserted in center comes out clean. Remove and cool on cake rack, just until warm. Prepare frosting while cake is cooling. Heat remaining ingredients in saucepan. Stir to blend. When frosting is well mixed and glossy, pour over warm cake. Makes 10 to 12 servings.

CARROT CAKE

2 cups all-purpose flour
2 teaspoons baking powder
1½ teaspoons baking soda
1 teaspoon salt
2½ teaspoons cinnamon
2 cups sugar
1½ cups vegetable oil
4 eggs, beaten
2 cups grated raw carrots
1 8-ounce can crushed pineapple, drained
1 cup chopped pecans
¼ cup Jack Daniel's Whiskey
Heavenly Frosting

Preheat oven to 350°. Sift together flour, baking powder, soda, salt and cinnamon. Mix together sugar, oil and eggs; add to flour mixture. Stir in carrots, pineapple, pecans and Jack Daniel's Whiskey. Bake in greased and floured 9x13-inch cake pan for 35 to 40 minutes or until a tester inserted in center comes out clean. Cool and frost with Heavenly Frosting. Makes 12 to 14 servings.

HEAVENLY FROSTING

1 stick butter, softened
8 ounces cream cheese, softened
1 tablespoon Jack Daniel's Whiskey
1 16-ounce box confectioners' sugar, sifted

In mixer, combine butter, cream cheese and Jack Daniel's Whiskey, until well blended. Add sugar gradually; beat vigorously. If too thick, add a small amount of Jack Daniel's Whiskey to thin to desired consistency.

CHOCOLATE SOUFFLÉ CAKE

8 ounces semi-sweet chocolate
7 egg yolks, at room temperature
⅔ cup sugar
⅓ cup finely ground toasted pecans
2 tablespoons strong brewed coffee
3½ tablespoons Jack Daniel's Whiskey
8 egg whites
Cocoa or confectioners' sugar
Whipped cream
Pecan halves

Preheat oven to 350°. Prepare 10-inch tube pan by buttering and dusting with confectioners' sugar. Melt chocolate in top of double boiler over simmering water. Remove from heat. Beat egg yolks with electric mixer. Slowly add all but 2 tablespoons sugar, beating until mixture is fluffy and forms a ribbon when beaters are lifted (about 5 minutes). Gradually blend in chocolate, pecans, coffee

and Jack Daniel's Whiskey. Whip egg whites until soft peaks form. Gradually add remaining sugar, beating whites until stiff but not dry. Gently fold ¼ of the whites into chocolate mixture. Then fold chocolate mixture into remaining whites. Pour into prepared pan. Bake until cake is puffed, top is dry, or until tester inserted in center comes out almost clean, about 35 to 40 minutes. Transfer to wire rack and cool in pan for about 1 hour. Invert cake onto serving platter. Sift cocoa or confectioners' sugar decoratively over top of cake. Before serving, pipe whipped cream around edges. Decorate with pecan halves. Makes 10 to 12 servings.

Tennessee Hospitality Cake

8 ounces raisins
2 sticks butter
1 16-ounce box confectioners' sugar, sifted
6 eggs, separated

4 cups all-purpose flour
½ teaspoon baking soda
1 teaspoon baking powder
1 tablespoon allspice
¾ cup Jack Daniel's Whiskey
½ cup molasses
8 ounces dates, chopped
2 cups chopped pecans

Preheat oven to 325°. Plump raisins in hot water and set aside. Cream butter and sugar until light and fluffy. Add egg yolks, one at a time, beating well after each addition. Sift dry ingredients together; add alternately with Jack Daniel's Whiskey and molasses. Stir in drained raisins, dates and pecans. Pour into 10-inch tube pan lined with greased foil. Bake for 45 to 50 minutes or until a tester inserted in center comes out clean. Makes 10 to 12 servings.

Grated Sweet Potato Cake

3 cups all-purpose flour
2 cups sugar
2 teaspoons baking powder
1 teaspoon baking soda
¼ teaspoon salt
2 teaspoons cinnamon
1 cup vegetable oil
1 15¼-ounce can crushed pineapple, undrained
2 teaspoons vanilla
3 eggs
2 cups grated raw sweet potatoes
1 cup toasted and chopped pecans
Tennessee Whiskey Sauce (see page 143)

Preheat oven to 350°. Stir together dry ingredients. In an electric mixer, combine dry ingredients, oil, pineapple and vanilla. Add eggs one at a time; beat well after each addition. Fold in sweet potatoes and nuts. Pour into greased and floured 10-inch tube pan. Bake for 1 hour 15 minutes. Serve with Tennessee Whiskey Sauce. Makes 10 to 12 servings.

TENNESSEE TODDY CAKE

1½ cups firmly packed light brown sugar
1 cup sugar
1 cup butter, softened
6 eggs, separated
4 cups cake flour, divided
4 teaspoons baking powder
½ teaspoon allspice
½ teaspoon nutmeg
½ teaspoon cinnamon
⅔ cup Jack Daniel's Whiskey
½ cup molasses
2½ cups golden raisins
1 cup chopped dried apricots
1 cup chopped dates
3 cups chopped pecans

Preheat oven to 325°. With an electric mixer, beat sugars and butter until light and fluffy. Beat in egg yolks. Combine 3 cups flour, baking powder and spices. Combine Jack Daniel's Whiskey and molasses. Add flour mixture to butter mixture alternately with whiskey mixture. Mix remaining cup flour with fruit and nuts. Fold in fruit and nuts. Beat remaining egg whites until stiff but not dry; fold into batter. Pour into 2 tube pans that have been greased and lined with wax paper. Bake for 1 hour or until a tester inserted in center comes out clean. Cool on wire rack for 3 minutes before removing from pans. Makes 2 cakes.

PRUNE CAKE AND BUTTERMILK SAUCE

2 cups all-purpose flour
1½ cups sugar
1 teaspoon baking soda
1 teaspoon salt
1 teaspoon cinnamon
1 teaspoon allspice
1 teaspoon nutmeg
1 teaspoon cocoa

3 eggs, beaten
1 cup vegetable oil
1 cup buttermilk
1 teaspoon vanilla
1 cup chopped stewed prunes
Buttermilk Sauce

Preheat oven to 325°. Sift together dry ingredients. In a large bowl, beat together eggs, oil, buttermilk and vanilla. Add dry ingredients. Stir in prunes. Pour into a greased and floured 10-inch tube pan. Bake for 50 to 55 minutes or until a tester inserted in center comes out clean. Cool in pan 15 minutes before turning out. Serve with Buttermilk Sauce. Makes 10 to 12 servings.

BUTTERMILK SAUCE

1 cup sugar
½ cup buttermilk
½ cup butter
1 tablespoon white corn syrup
½ teaspoon baking soda
½ teaspoon vanilla

Combine all ingredients in a saucepan. Bring to a boil and boil for 2 minutes. Serve warm over Prune Cake. Makes 2½ cups.

JACK DANIEL'S PUMPKIN PIE

1 20-ounce can pumpkin
¾ cup sugar
⅛ teaspoon powdered cloves
¼ teaspoon salt
½ teaspoon cinnamon
3 eggs, beaten
⅓ cup Jack Daniel's Whiskey
1 9-inch unbaked pie crust

Preheat oven to 350°. Place pumpkin in chilled mixing bowl. With the mixer going, slowly add the dry ingredients, beaten eggs and Jack Daniel's Whiskey, in that order. Pour pumpkin mixture into unbaked pie crust. Place in oven; after 30 minutes,

Beat egg yolks in mixer until light and fluffy, about 8 to 10 minutes; add sugar and continue beating until well blended. Soften gelatin in water; dissolve in pan over low heat. Cool. Stir Jack Daniel's Whiskey into lukewarm gelatin, then add to egg mixture. Whip cream until stiff; fold into egg mixture. Pour into prepared pie crust. Chill until filling is firm. Sprinkle pie *generously* with grated chocolate or chocolate curls (this adds to the flavor of the pie). Makes 6 to 8 servings.

JACK DANIEL'S CHOCOLATE CHIP PECAN PIE

By Robert Zielinski, Executive Pastry Chef, The Mansion on Turtle Creek, Dallas, Texas.

3 extra-large eggs, lightly beaten
1 cup sugar
2 tablespoons unsalted butter, melted
1 cup dark corn syrup
1 teaspoon vanilla
¼ cup Jack Daniel's Whiskey
½ cup semi-sweet chocolate morsels
1 cup whole pecans
1 10-inch pie crust

Preheat oven to 375°. Combine eggs, sugar, butter, syrup, vanilla and Jack Daniel's Whiskey. Mix well then strain. Sprinkle chocolate chips over the bottom of the unbaked pie crust; cover with pecans. Pour filling over chips and pecans. Bake for 35 to 40 minutes or until a knife inserted halfway between the center and the edge comes out clean. Set aside for at least 30 minutes before cutting. Makes 6 to 8 servings.

cover crusts with foil to prevent over-browning. Bake 30 minutes longer. Reset oven to 400° and bake an additional 8 to 10 minutes. *Note:* Pie will be darker in color than most pumpkin pies and has a tendency to pull away from the crust after it has cooled. The latter can be concealed by decorating or trimming with whipped cream. Makes 6 to 8 servings.

GOLD MEDAL CHIFFON PIE

3 egg yolks
½ cup sugar
1 tablespoon gelatin
¼ cup water
¼ cup Jack Daniel's Whiskey
1 cup heavy cream
1 9-inch graham cracker crust
Grated chocolate or chocolate curls

CHOCOLATE ALMOND PIE

  1 large (4½ ounces) chocolate almond candy bar
  ¼ cup milk
  1½ pints (1 jar) marshmallow creme
  1 cup heavy cream, whipped
  ½ teaspoon vanilla
  1 9-inch graham cracker crumb crust, chilled
    Chocolate curls
    Whole almonds

Combine chocolate and milk over low heat until melted. Add marshmallow creme to chocolate mixture and blend until smooth and creamy. Remove from heat. Fold in whipped cream. Pour into chilled crust; refrigerate. Garnish with chocolate curls and whole almonds. Makes 6 to 8 servings.

CONFEDERATE PIE

There are conflicting stories about how the following recipe got its name. The first story goes this way. During the Civil War the South raised up their own government and called themselves the Confederacy. The Federal government in Washington and the states that made up the Union never recognized the Southern establishment. Therefore, they always referred to the Confederacy as fake, or not what it presented itself to be. However, in the South the story is told in an altogether different light. During the war, food was in short supply for the Confederate Army, so army cooks did what they could with what they had on hand to make interesting meals. One item that they had plenty of was crackers. Because of this it was natural for a pie to be made from crackers and naturally be called Confederate Pie. Either explanation could be true, but the resulting pie is still just as good as it ever was.

  1½ cups sugar
  2 cups water
  2 tablespoons cream of tartar
    Butter

  22 saltine crackers
  1 9-inch unbaked pie crust
    Cinnamon

Preheat oven to 450°. Combine sugar, water, cream of tartar and 2 tablespoons butter. Boil for 2 minutes. Add crackers. Do not stir. Pour gently into pie crust. Dot with butter and sprinkle generously with cinnamon. Bake for 20 minutes. Looks and tastes exactly like apple pie. Makes 6 to 8 servings.

STEAMBOAT PIE

Before cookbooks were available to country or city folk, the exchange or sharing of recipes was the accepted and established way of increasing variety and imaginative table fare. Mothers, grandmothers, aunts, neighbors, and friends shared their favorites with a new bride to help her learn and prepare food for her new household. Receipts, as they were referred to, were as prized as new pots, pans, dishes and utensils for her new kitchen.

As manufacturers became more competitive in their advertising, recipes using their products were written on the cans or packages.

Although most day-to-day preparations such as biscuits, cornbread, pot roast and gravy were accomplished without the use of written receipts, special dishes were prepared from careful and accurate directions. Generations later these are still prized and shared.

One such surviving recipe prepared by ladies in this neck-of-the-woods is Steamboat Pie.

  1 cup firmly packed brown sugar
  3 eggs, slightly beaten
  1 cup light corn syrup
  1 teaspoon vanilla
  2 tablespoons melted butter
    Dash of salt
  1½ cups chopped pecans
  1 9-inch unbaked pie crust
  1 cup heavy cream
  1 tablespoon confectioners' sugar
  1 tablespoon Jack Daniel's Whiskey

Preheat oven to 400°. Blend first 6 ingredients, then stir in chopped pecans. Pour into unbaked pie crust. Bake for 10 minutes. Reduce temperature to 325° and bake for 30 minutes longer. Cool. To prepare topping, beat cream until stiff; adding confectioners' sugar and Jack Daniel's Whiskey. Place a dollop of topping on each slice of pie. Makes 6 to 8 servings.

GERMAN CHOCOLATE PIE

    1½ cups sugar
     2 tablespoons cocoa
     1 teaspoon cornstarch
     2 tablespoons all-purpose flour
    ¼ teaspoon salt
    ½ tablespoon butter, softened
    ¼ cup hot water
     2 eggs
     1 cup evaporated milk
    2¼ ounces (⅔ cup) coconut
     1 cup pecans, broken
     1 9-inch unbaked pie crust

Preheat oven to 350°. Combine dry ingredients. Add butter and water; mix well. Add eggs, milk, coconut and pecans; mix well. Pour into unbaked pie crust. Bake until center is firm. Makes 6 to 8 servings.

FESTIVE FALL PIE

In the fall of the year everyone takes their prize baked goods to the State Fair for judging. This festive pie is a winner anytime you serve it.

    ½ cup melted butter
     1 cup sugar
     3 eggs, beaten
    ½ cup flaked coconut
    ½ cup chopped pecans
    ½ cup chopped dates
     1 tablespoon vinegar
     1 9-inch unbaked pie crust

Preheat oven to 350°. Combine butter, sugar and eggs in bowl; mix well. Stir in coconut, pecans, dates and vinegar. Pour into unbaked pie crust. Bake for 1 hour and 15 minutes. Cool before serving. Makes 6 to 8 servings.

Maple Nut Pie

1 15-ounce can sweetened condensed milk
  Maple syrup
2 eggs
2 cups chopped pecans or walnuts
1 9-inch baked pie crust
  Whipped cream

Empty milk into saucepan. Fill milk can with maple syrup and combine with milk. Beat eggs and add to mixture. Cook slowly until thickened. Add pecans and pour into pie crust. Cool. Top with whipped cream if desired. Makes 6 to 8 servings.

Uncle Jack's Peach Pie

1 recipe cobbler pastry
1/4 cup butter
4 cups peeled, sliced peaches
1/2 cup firmly packed light brown sugar
1 1/2 teaspoons cinnamon
1/4 teaspoon grated nutmeg
1 1/4 cups cream
1/2 cup Jack Daniel's Whiskey
2 tablespoons sugar

Make pastry from favorite recipe and chill. Preheat oven to 350°. Melt butter in heavy saucepan. Add peaches, brown sugar, spices and cream. Bring to a boil and simmer for 5 minutes. Stir carefully to avoid crushing peaches. Add Jack Daniel's Whiskey; continue to cook for 15 minutes or until mixture is thickened. Remove from heat. Line baking pan with half the rolled-out pastry. Pour in peach filling. Cover with remaining pastry; prick with a fork to allow steam to escape during cooking. Sprinkle with 2 tablespoons sugar. Bake for 40 to 45 minutes or until lightly brown. (If edge of crust is browning too quickly, place a protective rim of foil lightly over it.)

Raisin Custard Pie

1 cup sugar
1/2 cup butter, softened
2 egg yolks, beaten
1/2 cup raisins
1/2 teaspoon allspice
1/2 teaspoon cinnamon
1/4 teaspoon salt
1 1/2 teaspoons vinegar
2 egg whites, stiffly beaten
1 teaspoon vanilla
1 9-inch unbaked pie crust

Preheat oven to 300°. Cream sugar and butter in mixer. Add egg yolks, raisins, spices, salt and vinegar. Blend well. Fold in stiffly beaten egg whites and vanilla. Pour into unbaked pie crust. Bake until firm, about 25 to 30 minutes. Top will be golden brown. Makes 6 to 8 servings.

Custard Chess Pie

1 9-inch pie crust
1 1/2 cups sugar
1/2 cup butter
4 eggs
1 tablespoon all-purpose flour
1/3 cup cream
3 tablespoons Jack Daniel's Whiskey

Preheat oven to 450°. Bake pie crust for 8 to 10 minutes. Remove from oven and lower heat to 350°. Cream sugar and butter until fluffy. Add eggs, flour, cream and Jack Daniel's Whiskey. Fill the partially baked pie shell. Bake pie for 50 to 55 minutes or until firm. Cool before cutting. Makes 6 to 8 servings.

UNBELIEVABLE PIE

1 unbaked graham cracker crust
½ cup chopped toasted pecans
1 ounce semi-sweet chocolate
½ cup butter
1 cup sugar
2 eggs, well beaten
  Whipped cream or ice cream

Preheat oven to 350°. Sprinkle nuts on bottom of graham cracker crust and set aside. Combine chocolate and butter in double boiler over simmering water. Stir until chocolate is melted. Remove from heat; whisk in sugar. Beat small amount of warmed chocolate into eggs. Add to chocolate mixture; and pour into crust. Bake until filling is puffed, about 25 minutes. Serve warm with whipped cream or ice cream. Makes 6 to 8 servings.

SINNER'S ANGEL PIE

1 cup graham cracker crumbs
1½ cups chopped and toasted pecans
1 cup semi-sweet chocolate morsels
1½ teaspoons baking powder
5 large egg whites, at room temperature
1 cup sugar
1 tablespoon Jack Daniel's Whiskey

Preheat oven to 325°. Combine crumbs, nuts, chocolate morsels and baking powder. Beat egg whites until foamy; gradually add sugar until all is used. Add Jack Daniel's Whiskey. Fold crumb mixture gently into egg whites. Spoon into greased and floured 10-inch (6-cup) glass pie pan. Bake for 35 to 40 minutes. Makes 6 to 8 servings.

Note: A glaze may be made to drizzle over pie by melting 2 tablespoons chocolate morsels with ½ tablespoon Jack Daniel's Whiskey and 1 teaspoon water. Serve with whipping cream.

OLD-FASHIONED CUSTARD PIE

1 9-inch pie crust
4 eggs
½ cup sugar
½ teaspoon salt
1 teaspoon vanilla
2 cups milk, scalded
  Nutmeg

Preheat oven to 400°. Partially bake crust for 5 to 8 minutes (mash bubbles down with the back of a spoon). Remove from oven. Combine eggs, sugar, salt and vanilla. Gradually stir in scalded milk. Pour into pie shell. Sprinkle with nutmeg. Bake at 400° for 15 minutes; reduce heat to 350° and continue baking for 15 to 20 minutes or until knife inserted in center comes out clean. Cool before serving. Makes 6 to 8 servings.

The Great American Celebration

. . . .

From grand hometown events to small family weekend gatherings, reunions and homecomings spell the spirit of Tennessee best. The love of grand scale socializing and visiting, combined with an abundance of wonderful food, makes these our favorite celebrations.

The invitation usually is initiated by some older member who has had a lot experience in reunions. Children are growing and old folks are departing. It is time to get together and catch up on what is going on with those we love.

Reunions give us an opportunity to think again of the good times we had when we were young, to re-tell the stories of when we were carefree and responsibilities didn't weight so heavy. It is a time to think about when the bloom of childhood was still in our faces and our bodies, and to hear that we 'haven't changed a bit.' My, that's nice to hear!

It is also a time to get things into perspective, to find that there are still honest folk, salt-of-the-earth folk, unchanged by time and times. Then there is the shock of finding out how things shrink as we get older. Remember how *big* the old homeplace, how *tall* the peach and apple trees you climbed, how *wide* the old creek and how *huge* the church sanctuary all were?

Next to conversation, the really big event is the eating. Everyone comes laden down with homemade pickles, salads and slaws, vegetable dishes, fried chicken, country ham, pork ribs and country-fried steak. Then there are the desserts; freezers of ice cream and sherbet, cobblers and pies. Southerners, and especially Tennesseans, are pie-eaters. Then all of the show-offs in the crowd have brought the most beautiful cakes . . . chocolate or white, devils food or angel food, pound or spice. This is the only time a show-off is truly appreciated and universally applauded!

Why are reunions such a favored celebration! If the truth were known, the big reason would be to see if the food is still as good back home as you tell everyone it is. And then you find out that some things really never change.

Old-Fashioned Lemon Cream Pie

1 cup sugar, divided
3 tablespoons all-purpose flour
1½ cups buttermilk
2 tablespoons butter
3 eggs, separated and at room temperature
1 tablespoon grated lemon rind
3 tablespoons lemon juice
1 baked 9-inch pie crust

Combine ¾ cup sugar and flour in heavy saucepan. Stir in buttermilk; mix well and cook over medium heat, stirring constantly, until mixture comes to a boil. Remove from heat and stir in butter. Beat egg yolks. Gradually add to hot mixture, stirring constantly. Remove from heat and stir in lemon rind and juice. Pour immediately into pie crust. Preheat oven to 375°. Beat egg whites at high speed with an electric mixer for 1 minute. Gradually add ¼ cup sugar, one tablespoon at a time, beating until stiff peaks form. Spread over warm filling; seal edges of pastry. Bake for 10 minutes or until the meringue is lightly browned. Cool and serve. Makes 6 to 8 servings.

Lincoln County's Black Jack Pie

1 9-inch baked pie crust
⅔ cup sugar
⅓ cup cornstarch
¼ teaspoon salt
3 cups milk
3 eggs, separated
1 tablespoon butter
2 teaspoons vanilla
4 tablespoons cocoa
9 tablespoons sugar, divided
2 tablespoons Jack Daniel's Whiskey

Prepare pie crust and cool. Combine next four ingredients in saucepan. Separate eggs (reserve whites for meringue). Beat egg yolks and add to ingredients in saucepan; blend well. Stir mixture over medium heat until it boils. Stir and boil for 1 minute, being careful not to let it burn. Remove from heat and stir in butter and vanilla. Combine cocoa, 3 tablespoons sugar and Jack Daniel's Whiskey; add to filling. Return to heat, stirring constantly, just until it starts to boil again. Remove from heat; pour into prepared pie crust. Preheat oven to 350°. While pie is still hot, beat egg whites until foamy. Gradually add 6 tablespoons of sugar and beat until stiff. Spread meringue over pie, carefully sealing edges to crust. Bake for 8 minutes or until golden brown. Cool. Makes 6 to 8 servings.

Lemon Rub Pie

1¾ cups sugar
2 tablespoons cornmeal
1 tablespoon all-purpose flour
4 eggs, lightly beaten

¼ cup melted butter
¼ cup milk
¼ cup lemon juice
2 tablespoons grated lemon rind
1 9-inch unbaked pie crust

Preheat oven to 375°. Combine sugar, cornmeal and flour. Add eggs, butter, milk, lemon juice and rind; mix well. Pour into unbaked pie crust. Bake for 35 to 40 minutes or until lightly browned on top. Cool. Makes 6 to 8 servings.

OL' SOUTH MACAROON PIE

1 stick butter, softened
6 eggs
2 cups sugar
2½ cups milk
¼ cup all-purpose flour
2 cups flaked coconut
1 teaspoon vanilla
Dash of salt

Preheat oven to 350°. Cream butter and eggs; add sugar, mixing until light and fluffy. Add remaining ingredients; blend well. Pour into 2 8-inch pie pans. Bake for 35 to 40 minutes. (Pie will make its own crust.) Makes 6 to 8 servings per pie.

MAGGIE'S 'LASSES PIE

1 cup sugar
3 eggs
1 tablespoon milk
3 tablespoons melted butter
1 cup molasses or dark corn syrup
1 teaspooon vanilla
1 9-inch unbaked pie crust

Preheat oven to 400°. With mixer, blend sugar, eggs and milk. Add butter, molasses and vanilla. Blend well. Pour into unbaked pie crust. Bake for 10 minutes. Reduce heat to 350° and bake for 50 minutes or until firm. Cool. Makes 6 to 8 servings.

AUNT DOROTHY'S BEST CUSTARD PIE

4 eggs, slightly beaten
½ cup sugar
¼ teaspoon salt
½ teaspoon vanilla
2 teaspoons lemon extract
2½ cups milk, scalded
1 9-inch unbaked pie crust
Nutmeg

Preheat oven to 350°. Blend eggs, sugar, salt, vanilla and lemon extracts. Gradually stir into scalded milk. Pour into unbaked crust. Sprinkle top with nutmeg. Bake for 45 to 60 minutes or until pie is golden brown and eggs are set. Cool. Makes 6 to 8 servings.

Tipsy Mud Pie

1 15-ounce package cream-filled chocolate cookies
6 tablespoons butter, melted
1 tablespoon instant coffee granules
¼ cup Jack Daniel's Whiskey
1 cup heavy cream
1 pint chocolate ice cream, softened
¼ cup lightly toasted and chopped pecans
2 tablespoons chocolate syrup

In a food processor, use steel blade to chop cookies into fine crumbs. Add melted butter and press into a 10-inch pie pan. Place in freezer to harden. Stir coffee into Jack Daniel's Whiskey until dissolved. Whip cream until stiff. Fold in coffee mixture. Fold ½ the mixture into softened ice cream; spread into pie crust. Cover and freeze overnight. Before serving, spread remaining whipped cream over top. Sprinkle with pecans; drizzle on chocolate syrup to garnish. Makes 8 servings.

Eggnog Pie

1 29-ounce can fruit cocktail in syrup
1 envelope unflavored gelatin
1½ cups prepared eggnog
¼ teaspoon salt
⅛ teaspoon vanilla
¼ teaspoon almond flavoring
1 cup heavy cream
1 9-inch baked pie crust or graham cracker crust

Drain fruit cocktail thoroughly, reserving syrup. Measure ½ cup of syrup; stir gelatin into syrup in top of double boiler over simmering water. Stir until gelatin is dissolved. Remove from heat and stir in eggnog. Add salt and flavorings. Chill until mixture mounds when dropped from a spoon. Whip cream and fold into gelatin mixture along with 1½ cups fruit cocktail. Chill again for 10 minutes. Heap into prepared pie crust; chill for 2 to 4 hours. Makes 6 to 8 servings.

OL' FASHIONED CHEESE PIE

1 16-ounce carton cream-style cottage cheese
3 eggs
⅔ cup sugar
2 teaspoons lemon juice
¼ cup Jack Daniel's Whiskey
1 tablespoon grated lemon peel
1 9-inch unbaked pie crust

Preheat oven to 425°. In mixing bowl, beat first 6 ingredients on medium-high speed for 4 minutes, scraping sides often. Pour into unbaked pie crust and bake at 425° for 10 minutes. Reduce heat to 350°; bake for 30 to 35 minutes longer. Cool. Makes 6 to 8 servings.

BUTTERMILK PIE

The sweet one in a kitchen is the one who concocts delicious desserts. Louise Gregory is the dessert cook at Miss Bobo's Boarding House. She creates heavenly custards, flaky pie crusts, delectable fillings and mile-high meringues. Luscious cakes or pies are all wonderful when prepared by Louise. Here she shares an old country custard favorite, Buttermilk Pie.

1¼ cups sugar
2 tablespoons cornmeal
3 eggs, beaten
½ cup butter, melted
⅓ cup buttermilk
1 teaspoon vanilla
1 9-inch unbaked pie crust

Preheat oven to 350°. Stir sugar and cornmeal together. Add eggs, butter, buttermilk and vanilla; blend well. Pour into pie crust. Bake 40 to 45 minutes or until set. Cool to room temperature before serving. Makes 6 servings.

SURPRISING MERINGUE PIE

3 egg whites at room temperature
Dash of salt
1 teaspoon almond extract
1 cup sugar
¾ cup soda cracker crumbs
½ teaspoon baking powder
¾ cup lightly toasted and chopped pecans
Whipped cream
Maraschino cherries

Preheat oven to 325°. In an electric mixer, beat egg whites until foamy. Add salt and almond extract. Gradually beat in sugar one tablespoonful at a time. Stir together crumbs, baking powder and nuts. When meringue is shiny and stiff, fold in crumb mixture. Spoon into a greased and floured pie pan. Bake for 30 to 35 minutes or until lightly browned. Cool before cutting. Top slices with whipped cream and a cherry. Makes 6 to 8 servings.

CITRUS CHIFFON PIE

1 envelope unflavored gelatin
½ cup sugar
    Dash of salt
4 egg yolks
½ cup lemon juice
½ cup orange juice
¼ cup water
½ teaspoon grated lemon rind
½ teaspoon grated orange rind
4 egg whites
⅓ cup sugar
1 9-inch baked pie crust

Whipped cream
Orange slices

Mix gelatin, ½ cup sugar and salt in saucepan. Beat together egg yolks, juices and water. Stir into gelatin mixture. Cook over medium heat, stirring constantly, just until mixture comes to a boil. Remove from heat; stir in rinds. Chill, stirring occasionally, until mixture mounds slightly when dropped from a spoon. Beat egg whites until soft peaks form. Gradually add ⅓ cup sugar; beat until stiff peaks form. Fold in gelatin mixture. Pile into cooled pie crust. Chill until firm. Garnish with whipped cream and thinly sliced oranges.

ACCOMPANIMENTS

GLAZE FOR ROAST HAM

1 cup orange juice
¼ cup Jack Daniel's Whiskey
½ cup brown sugar
1 tablespoon powdered ginger
½ teaspoon whole cloves

Combine ingredients and bring to a boil. Reduce heat and simmer about 30 minutes or until syrup-like consistency. Brush over ham several times during last hour of baking. Makes 1½ cups.

MAYFAIR DRESSING

1 clove garlic
1 rib celery
½ medium onion
1 2-ounce can flat anchovies, drained
1 teaspoon ground pepper
1 heaping teaspoon Accent
½ teaspoon sugar
2 tablespoons mustard
1 tablespoon lemon juice
3 eggs
2 cups vegetable oil

Peel and mince garlic. Scrape and slice celery. Peel and slice onion. Place in blender or food processor; add all remaining ingredients except eggs and oil. Process for a few seconds. Add eggs; blend for a few more seconds. Add oil, ¼ cup at a time, blending between each addition. Blend a few seconds longer after all the oil has been added. This keeps well for 2 weeks or longer in the refrigerator. Use on romaine, spinach, and head lettuce. Garnish salad with croutons. Makes 1 quart.

Bleu Cheese Dressing

¼ cup red wine vinegar
1 teaspoon salt
⅛ teaspoon freshly ground pepper
½ teaspoon Worcestershire sauce
1½ teaspoons grated onion
1 cup olive oil
¾ cup mayonnaise
½ cup (2 ounces) bleu cheese, crumbled

Combine vinegar, salt, pepper, Worcestershire sauce and onion. Gradually whisk in olive oil. Then whisk in mayonnaise until smooth. Add crumbled cheese. Makes 2½ cups.

Intense Applesauce

5 cups apple cider
6 large cooking apples, peeled, cored and cut into chunks
3 tablespoons firmly packed light brown sugar
3 tablespoons butter
1 teaspoon cinnamon

Boil the cider until reduced by half. Add apple slices and lower heat. Simmer, covered, for about 40 minutes or until apples are tender; stir occasionally to prevent sticking. Add sugar, butter and cinnamon; blend until sugar is dissolved. Mash with a potato masher, leaving some apple chunks. If sauce is too thin, continue cooking over low heat until thickened. Makes 3 cups.

Sauced Applesauce

¼ cup butter
3 Red Delicious apples, chopped
1 onion, chopped
⅓ cup Jack Daniel's Whiskey, warmed
2 cups chicken stock
⅓ cup heavy cream

Melt butter in heavy skillet. Sauté apples and onion until tender. Pour warmed Jack Daniel's Whiskey over apples and carefully ignite. When flame goes out, add chicken stock; simmer for several minutes. Add cream and reduce sauce until it begins to thicken. This is delicious with pork.

Banana Pancakes

1 egg
1 tablespoon sugar
3 tablespoons all-purpose flour
½ teaspoon baking powder
Dash of salt
3 ripe bananas, mashed
Confectioners' sugar

Beat egg with sugar. Add flour, baking powder, salt and bananas. Stir just until blended. Drop a tablespoon of batter at a time onto a greased griddle or skillet. Turn when bubbles appear. Watch closely; they cook quickly. Sprinkle with confectioners' sugar to serve. Makes 14 to 16 small pancakes.

The Art of Tall Tales

W hen growing up, we probably never thought about storytelling as an *art,* but everyone knew who the good storytellers in the family were. They just naturally drew a crowd at family get-togethers or after dinner on the porch or in the park on Sunday afternoons. They could take a mundane, everyday, no 'count happening and describe it as if it were the greatest event in the country. These experts at their art knew when to pause, when to punctuate, when to embellish and when to elaborate. They could move you with the depth of an evangelist or soothe you with the peace of a river. Any way you looked at it, their stories were ornaments of beauty.

Somewhere between *remember when* and today, the art of storytelling has diminished. Maybe the abundance of books, radio, movies and television has eliminated our need to entertain and be entertained by this timeless art. But now it is in a revival. Tennessee's National Storytelling Festival in Jonesborough each year draws huge crowds to hear the tales of the mountain men, the wyooter and feats of glory from Tennessee's own.

Tall tale tellers from Tennessee are once again known by the crowds that gather at their knees and thrill to the magic of a story as the storyteller spins a web of delight.

GIBLET GRAVY

    3 cups water
    1 teaspoon salt
      Giblets from turkey
      Turkey neck
    6 tablespoons all-purpose flour
    ½ cup water
    3 hard-boiled eggs, sliced
      Salt and pepper to taste

Combine water with 1 teaspoon salt; add giblets and turkey neck. Cover and cook over medium heat until tender, about 1½ hours. Remove meat from broth, discard neck; chop giblets and return to broth. Blend flour with water to form a smooth paste; stir into broth. Cook, stirring constantly until thickened. Add sliced eggs and season with salt and pepper. Serve over cornbread dressing and turkey. Makes 3 cups.

SAUCE ANDALOUSE

    4 medium tomatoes
    ½ red bell pepper, seeded or 4 ounces canned pimientos, drained
    1 teaspoon vegetable oil
    1 teaspoon fresh tarragon, minced
    1 teaspoon fresh parsley, minced
    2 cups mayonnaise (homemade is best)
      Salt to taste

Peel, seed and mince tomatoes; add red pepper. Cook in oil over *lowest* heat for 1½ hours or until sauce is reduced to ¾ cup. Stir occasionally. Remove from heat and stir in spices. Cool. Fold in mayonnaise. This may be refrigerated for up to 2 weeks. This is delicious with cold chicken and poached salmon. Use instead of mayonnaise in shrimp or potato salads. Makes 2½ cups.

SPECIAL PIMIENTO CHEESE

    1 4-ounce can pimientos, chopped, oil reserved
    ½ cup mayonnaise
    ¼ cup Durkee's sauce
    1 tablespoon Dijon-style mustard
    ⅛ teaspoon cayenne
    1 clove garlic, minced
    ⅓ cup finely chopped fresh parsley
    2 teaspoons sugar
    ½ pound grated mild cheddar cheese
    ½ pound grated processed American cheese

Combine all ingredients except cheeses. Add grated cheeses and mix well. Moisten with reserved pimiento oil. Chill overnight to ripen flavor. This is good on whole wheat bread. Makes 4 cups.

TENNESSEE TIPSY SAUCE

    4 tablespoons butter
    1 cup confectioners' sugar
    1 egg
    3 to 4 tablespoons Jack Daniel's Whiskey

Soften butter to room temperature; add sugar and egg, beating well. Add Jack Daniel's Whiskey to taste; chill for 2 hours before serving. Yields approximately 1½ cups.

Note: This Tipsy Sauce was developed by the Pepper Patch, an all-natural gourmet foods company, to top its Tennessee Tipsy Cake. The cake is rich with Jack Daniel's Whiskey and other wonderful ingredients. Dot Smith, president of the company, developed the cake in response to a request from then-Governor's wife, Honey Alexander, for a special Tennessee gift item to be presented from the governor to the other fifty-one state governors visiting Tennessee during their 1983 Governor's Conference. The cake was an outstanding success and is now marketed in specialty stores and gourmet food shops all over the United States.

Tennessee Praline Topping

½ cup butter
1 cup firmly packed light brown sugar
1 cup toasted and chopped pecans
2 tablespoons white corn syrup
¼ cup Jack Daniel's Whiskey

Combine butter, sugar, pecans, and syrup in skillet. Bring to a boil, stirring constantly. Reduce heat and simmer for 1 minute (do not overcook). Remove from heat; stir in Jack Daniel's Whiskey. Serve immediately over ice cream or cake. Makes 1½ cups.

Jack Daniel's Ice Cream Topping

1 tablespoon butter
¼ cup light corn syrup
2 tablespoons dark brown sugar
Pinch of cinnamon
⅛ teaspoon salt
¼ cup water
½ cup lightly toasted and chopped nuts
3 tablespoons Jack Daniel's Whiskey

Combine all ingredients in saucepan except nuts and Jack Daniel's Whiskey. Cook over medium heat until thick and syrupy. Remove from heat and stir in Jack Daniel's Whiskey and nuts. Serve warm. Makes 1 cup.

Spiked Pancake Syrup

1 cup maple syrup
2 tablespoons butter
3 tablespoons Jack Daniel's Whiskey

Combine all ingredients and heat until bubbly. Serve over hot pancakes or waffles. Makes 1¼ cups.

Plastered Hot Fudge Sauce

1 cup sugar
¾ cup unsweetened cocoa, sifted
1 teaspoon instant coffee granules
Dash of salt
2 tablespoons Jack Daniel's Whiskey
1 cup heavy cream
¼ cup butter

Combine sugar, cocoa, coffee and salt in saucepan. Mix Jack Daniel's Whiskey with cream; add to sauce and stir until sauce is smooth. Cook over medium heat, stirring constantly. When sugar has dissolved, add butter and cook until thickened, about 5 minutes. Serve warm. Makes 2 cups.

Fruit and Vegetable Relish

30 large ripe tomatoes, peeled
6 pears, peeled and cored
6 small onions
6 peaches, peeled and pitted
6 green peppers, seeded
3 cups sugar
2 tablespoons salt
2 cups vinegar
3 tablespoons mixed pickling spice, tied in cheesecloth

Coarsely chop all the fruit in a large wooden bowl if possible, so none of the juices are lost. Place in a large, heavy pot and add remaining ingredients. Bring to a boil and continue to cook briskly, over medium heat, uncovered, for about 2 hours, stirring often with a wooden spoon. Be careful not to let mixture stick to the bottom of the pan (reduce heat if necessary). When mixture is reduced and as thick as applesauce, the relish is done. Pour into hot sterilized jars, cover, seal and process. Delicious with grilled meat or scrambled eggs. Makes about 6 pints.

AMBER JACK MARMALADE

Elvie and Clarence Rolman made two trips to the land-down-under as goodwill ambassadors. Clarence, retired from Jack Daniel's Distillery, created quite a stir with his knowledge of whiskey making. The pronounced difference in his Tennessee twang-drawl and the Australian accent sometimes caused a little verbal tussle. For instance, an Australian recipe called "Outback Marmalade" was translated "Amber Jack Marmalade" when Elvie made it back home. The reason? The Australians use Jack Daniel's to make their marmalade. By either name, the results are the same . . . delicious!

4 medium oranges
Juice of two lemons
12 cups cold water
8 cups sugar
¼ cup Jack Daniel's Whiskey

Scrub oranges. Using a citrus zester or fine grater, strip rind from oranges. Squeeze juice from oranges and lemons; set aside in a large container. Coarsely chop orange pulp (discard seeds) and tie in a cheesecloth bag. Drop bag into juice container along with 12 cups of water and grated rind. Soak overnight. Discard cheesecloth bag. Transfer liquid and grated rind to a large pan; bring to a boil. Reduce heat; simmer for 1 hour. Add sugar; return to a boil and cook until mixture reaches 220° on a candy thermometer. Remove from heat. Skim off surface foam. Cool for 5 minutes; add Jack Daniel's Whiskey. Pour into hot, sterilized jelly glasses, cover, seal and process. Fills 6 to 8 jelly glasses.

TOMATO GRAVY

After frying pork chops, discard all but 2 tablespoons drippings (lard or oil) from the skillet.

¼ cup finely chopped onion
2 tablespoons all-purpose flour
2 cups tomatoes, peeled, seeded and chopped
Chicken stock
½ teaspoon powdered thyme
1 teaspoon sugar
Salt and pepper to taste

In the skillet with the reserved drippings, sauté onion until tender. Stir in flour; cook several minutes. Add tomatoes and stir well. Chicken stock or water may be needed, depending on the amount of liquid from the tomatoes. Season with thyme, sugar, salt and pepper. Cook over low heat, stirring often until thickened. Serve with rice and pork chops. Makes 2 cups.

COUNTRY HOT RELISH

2 tomatoes, chopped
1 small onion, minced
1 green pepper, minced
1 pod hot red or green pepper, seeded and finely
   minced (or substitute ½ teaspoon hot pepper sauce)
1½ tablespoons distilled white vinegar
⅓ cup water
1 tablespoon sugar
¼ teaspoon salt
⅛ teaspoon pepper

Combine all ingredients; blend well. Cover and chill until ready to serve. Any leftover sauce may be kept in the refrigerator for up to 1 week. This is a must with fresh green beans, pinto beans or crowder peas. Makes about 2½ cups, or 8 to 10 servings.

GREEN TOMATO MINCEMEAT

4 large green tomatoes, cored and chopped
4 large apples, peeled, cored and chopped
3 cups firmly packed light brown sugar
4 tablespoons butter
3 cups golden raisins
1 teaspoon ground cloves
1 teaspoon nutmeg
1 teaspoon ground cinnamon
1 cup apple cider vinegar
1 cup chopped English walnuts

Combine all ingredients except nuts. Simmer in heavy saucepan for 2 hours or until thickened. Remove from heat; add walnuts. Cool and refrigerate. This is delicious as a condiment with venison or other strong game. Or add some Jack Daniel's Whiskey and use as a filling for tarts or pies. Makes about 2½ quarts.

PENNSYLVANIA DUTCH CABBAGE RELISH

2 cups finely chopped cabbage
1 large finely chopped red bell pepper
1 large finely chopped green bell pepper
1 cup finely chopped celery
4 teaspoons salt
2 tablespoons mustard seed
3 tablespoons brown sugar
1 cup vinegar

Toss cabbage, peppers and celery with salt. Cover and chill overnight. Rinse and drain in a colander until all liquid is gone. Combine mustard seed and brown sugar with vinegar in a saucepan; bring to a boil. Pour over drained vegetables; chill overnight. Makes 3 cups.

QUICK CORN RELISH

1 12-ounce can whole kernel corn, drained (reserve ¼
   cup liquid)
1 small onion, thinly sliced
2 tablespoons chopped green pepper
2 tablespoons chopped pimiento
¼ cup vinegar
½ teaspoon cornstarch
¼ cup light brown sugar
½ teaspoon salt
¼ teaspoon mustard seed
½ teaspoon celery seed
¼ teaspoon red pepper sauce

In a small pan, combine reserved corn liquid with all ingredients, except corn. Bring to a boil; simmer 5 minutes. Remove from heat; stir in corn. Cool and refrigerate. Makes 2 cups.

INTOXICATED CRANBERRY RELISH

4 cups fresh cranberries
1 whole orange, quartered, seeds removed
1¾ cups sugar
3 tablespoons Jack Daniel's Whiskey

Using a food processor, with the metal blade in place, place half the cranberries and half the orange into container; chop until coarsely ground. Transfer to a large bowl. Repeat with remaining cranberries and orange pieces. Combine cranberry mixture with sugar and Jack Daniel's Whiskey. Store in covered container in refrigerator overnight for flavors to ripen. Makes 3½ cups.

OVERNIGHT CUCUMBERS

8 small cucumbers
2 onions
¼ cup sugar
¾ to 1 cup vinegar
1 teaspoon dill seed
1 teaspoon mustard seed
1 teaspooon celery seed
1 tablespooon salt
½ teaspooon cream of tartar

Peel and slice cucumbers and onions (remove seeds from cucumbers if large and tough). Boil remaining ingredients together for 1 minute; pour over vegetables. Marinate, covered, in refrigerator overnight. Makes 3 cups.

PICKLED FIRECRACKERS

3 cloves garlic
3 sprigs dill
3 hot peppers, long red ones
  Okra, young and tender, enough to fill jar
1 cup water
1 cup vinegar
1 tablespoon salt

Pack garlic, dill, peppers and okra tightly in a clean, hot quart jar. In stainless steel saucepan, bring remaining ingredients to a boil. Pour over okra. Cover jar; cool. Place in refrigerator to age for 3 to 4 weeks. Makes 1 quart.

PICKLED OKRA

2½ pounds very small okra pods, each 2 to 2½ inches long
6 cloves garlic, peeled
6 heads dill weed
12 dried red pepper pods
3 teaspoons mustard seeds
48 black peppercorns
5⅓ cups white vinegar
3¾ cups water
3 tablespoons salt

Rinse the okra in cold water and trim the stems (do not remove the caps). Pack the okra into six 1-pint dry, sterile jars alternating the blossom and stem ends. Divide the garlic, dill, pepper pods, mustard seed and peppercorns evenly among the 6 jars. Combine the vinegar, water and salt in a saucepan and bring to a boil. Pour the boiling brine over the okra to within ½-inch of the top of the jar. Process as for any pickle. Makes 6 pints.

INDEX

A

B

W

Z